CE

English Local Government Reformed

LORD REDCLIFFE-MAUD
BRUCE WOOD

English Local Government Reformed

OXFORD UNIVERSITY PRESS
London   Oxford   New York
1974

Oxford University Press, Ely House, London W.1

GLASGOW NEW YORK TORONTO MELBOURNE WELLINGTON
CAPE TOWN IBADAN NAIROBI DAR ES SALAAM LUSAKA ADDIS ABABA
DELHI BOMBAY CALCUTTA MADRAS KARACHI LAHORE DACCA
KUALA LUMPUR SINGAPORE HONG KONG TOKYO

PAPERBACK ISBN 0 19 888091 X
CASEBOUND ISBN 0 19 885091 3

© OXFORD UNIVERSITY PRESS 1974

PRINTED IN GREAT BRITAIN
BY HAZELL WATSON AND VINEY LTD
AYLESBURY, BUCKS

Preface

THIS is a new book. Its structure follows closely that of a book written by one of us forty years ago, *Local Government in England and Wales*.[1] But since 1953, when that book was brought up to date by Professor Finer, English local government has been under fairly continuous revision, culminating in a group of legislative acts which take effect on 1 April 1974 and make that date the start of a new chapter in the history not only of local government but of the national health and other services, especially those based on water.

This seems therefore the right time for a new book. We have set out to cover all the ground covered by the old one, except that we confine ourselves to England. Much of what we write is also true of Wales, and Parliament has now passed further legislation which will give Scotland something not unlike the system that England and Wales now have. But whereas the old book concerned itself hardly at all with history, we have started our study with the old structure existing twenty years ago and traced the process of its replacement by what exists today.

We wish to express our special thanks to Dr. J. M. Finnis, Fellow of University College, Oxford, and Rhodes Reader in the Laws of the British Commonwealth and the United States, for his invaluable help over the chapter on Local Government and the Courts. Though here, as elsewhere in the book, any errors are our sole responsibility, we must acknowledge a quite exceptional debt to him.

[1] By J. P. R. Maud, in the Home University Library (London, 1932); second edition 1953 by Sir John Maud and S. E. Finer.

We must also thank our secretaries for indispensable help in typing our successive drafts.

R.-M.
B. W.

Autumn 1973

Contents

List of Tables and Maps

1

Introduction

BETWEEN 1958 and 1974 the structure and working of English local government were under virtually continuous review. Government-sponsored inquiries resulted in a steady stream of official publications, passing judgement on most aspects of the system—the geographical structure, the distribution of functions between authorities, the financing of local government, and the internal working of elected councils.

The consequences for local government have been greater than in any period since the years between the creation of county councils in 1888 and parish and district councils in 1894. Parliament has passed laws changing the whole administrative map of England and reallocating responsibility for certain important public services, notably health and those concerning water. New laws have also affected the finances of local government, reduced the number of central government controls over local authorities, and introduced local 'ombudsmen' to investigate claims of maladministration. Finally, many local councils have themselves adopted a large number of recommendations about their internal organization and mode of work (here new laws were not necessary).

The main landmarks in this period of reappraisal can best be determined by considering three separate questions. First, why was there this intense official activity? Secondly, how were the several reviews conducted? And finally, what were their more important results?

WHY REAPPRAISE?

This question might suggest that at some moment in time the government of the day took a conscious decision to review comprehensively the local government system. No such decision was ever taken. The period of reappraisal was in fact characterized by a series of separate decisions, taken by different governments and ministers and by local authorities themselves. There was no conscious programme nor any clear logic behind the chain of events. Indeed it has often been argued that in 1964, for example, it was not sensible to set up a committee to review the internal management of local government in advance of decisions about local government structure: after all, the size and scale of activities of reorganized local councils might well make irrelevant earlier proposals about internal organization based on the structure of that time.

The one common thread running through the decisions to examine this or that aspect of local government was simply the alleged inadequacy of the system to cope with the growing demands made on it as governments continued to extend the range of public services and as conditions of daily life were transformed by the increasing mobility and size of the population. This inadequacy can itself be traced back through a series of decisions taken during the last hundred years.

Two principles which underpinned the twin Local Government Acts of 1888 and 1894 were of first importance. These acts established the structure of local government which lasted until 1974—county borough and county government, with district councils operating as a 'second tier' within counties. And the principles underlying these statutory provisions were, first, that all local authorities should be democratically elected and, secondly, that towns should be governed separately from rural areas. Thus large towns became county boroughs and remained wholly outside the control of county councils, while smaller towns became non-county boroughs or urban districts, as subdivisions of the county quite separate from rural districts, which in turn consisted of a number of villages each with its parish council or parish meeting.

The principle of local democracy remains as important today as in the period 1888–94, and many of the practical results continue to be disappointing. At post-war local elections, for example, as many as half of all county councillors and three-quarters of councillors in rural districts were normally returned unopposed. The number of electors troubling to vote dropped in this period to around one in three. Sample surveys showed that few citizens knew even the name of their councillor, let alone the range of services for which he was responsible. In 1964 one of the reasons for establishing the Maud Committee on Management was that the local authorities themselves felt concerned about these facts. The decision by Government and Parliament in 1972 to create local 'ombudsmen' to investigate cases of alleged maladministration was also taken because councillors were thought to be unable to handle all such cases. And the provisions in the 1972 Local Government Act for public and press access to committee meetings of local authorities reflected a common view that councils were taking too many decisions behind closed doors.

But it was the second principle—the distinction between urban and rural areas—that increasingly came to be seen as local government's major weakness. First, it accounted for the existence of many small authorities. Towns with a population of only 50,000 might become county boroughs under the provisions of the 1888 act, and many of these towns remained all-purpose authorities right up to 1974 despite their failure to grow much beyond 50,000 and despite the much wider range of services that needed provision. Secondly, it became more and more difficult to keep the boundaries of urban authorities in line with the physical edge of a town. The growth of suburbs made boundary extensions logically necessary, but county councils became increasingly unhappy at losing territory and resources to county boroughs, as did rural districts to boroughs and urban districts. Proposals for boundary extensions to county boroughs were therefore almost always strongly contested by counties and districts. Governments were reluctant to seek a radical solution to this problem, and local-authority boundaries in many areas became more and more obviously out of date. A cold war between authorities (particularly between counties and county boroughs) continued to develop until it could be checked only by the creation of a new structure of local government.

This problem of boundaries and boundary changes was important in its own right. It becomes of even greater significance when account is taken of the responsibilities of local authorities to provide an increasing number and range of public services. For while boundaries often remained static (particularly after legislation in 1926 and 1929 made changes in county borough areas virtually impossible), the range of functions entrusted to local government certainly did not. Nor did population. Nor did patterns of human behaviour, for the development of the internal combustion engine led to increased mobility and the growth of suburbs and quasi-suburbs. More and more people lived in the area of one local authority and worked in that of another.

Human mobility on such a scale clearly affected the provision of the traditional Victorian local government services of highways, sanitation, police, and fire protection. It also had an impact on new services such as land-use planning and the building of council houses. In addition, higher standards of living meant increased expectations of other new services such as education, health, and welfare. This meant that local authorities were being asked to provide a far wider range of services in a period of rapid social change but within a framework which remained relatively inflexible.

It may seem astonishing that radical change was so long delayed. The main explanation was fundamental British conservatism, seen at its most stubborn when people are asked their views about any change in local institutions. Secondly, British local governors have long shown remarkable capacity to compete against the odds and make the best of a bad structure by using their common sense. But, thirdly, there was the inherent difficulty of finding a new structure to meet the challenge of constantly accelerating social change. A serious attempt was in fact made towards the end of the last war.

Sir Malcolm Trustram Eve (later Lord Silsoe) was asked by the war-time Coalition Government to chair a commission which would recommend how boundaries should be brought up to date and local government enabled to tackle the tremendous tasks of post-war housing and reconstruction. The commission made an intensive review of the whole country. Its conclusion was inevitable: its terms of reference were too narrow; not only boundaries but functions must be changed. It therefore produced a plan to cover both: many of the county boroughs must be brought within the ambit of new and wider-ranging counties. But by 1948 when this plan was ready,[1] there was a Labour Government in office and the responsible minister, Aneurin Bevan, would have none of it. He set his ministry to work out an alternative plan, but the next general election so reduced the government majority that no reform of local government could be attempted. The Conservative Government,

---

[1] *Report of the Local Government Boundary Commission for the year 1947* (H.M.S.O., 1948).

returned in 1951, was in due course, but not immediately, compelled to take a new initiative.

HOW WAS THE REAPPRAISAL UNDERTAKEN?

An important feature of the re-examination of local government between 1958 and 1974 was the use made by successive governments of independent commissions or committees.

Five bodies of this kind paved the way for structural change. The first was the Royal Commission on Local Government in Greater London. Known as the Herbert Commission, after its chairman Sir Edwin Herbert (later Lord Tangley), it sat from 1957 to 1960 and considered the structure of local government in the metropolitan area.[2]

Two committees proved necessary for the rest of England. The first, the Local Government Commission for England, was created by the 1958 Local Government Act. It was to review county and county borough boundaries and consider whether a new structure was needed in the conurbations. However, before it completed its work it was replaced in 1966 by the Royal Commission on Local Government in England (the Redcliffe-Maud Commission). This reported in 1969.

Another commission was set up early in 1969 to consider, among other things, the possibility of regional government. This commission on the constitution was originally known as the Crowther Commission, but on the death of Lord Crowther in 1972 its chairman became Lord Kilbrandon. It reported in 1973.

Finally, under the 1972 Local Government Act a permanent new body was created to examine local boundaries and keep them under continuing review. The first task of this Local Government Boundary Commission was to draw up a scheme of county districts within the new counties.

These five bodies were used by various governments as an alternative to direct ministerial initiation of reform. It can fairly be argued that they all did valuable work in hearing witnesses and appraising large amounts of evidence which would not have been available to the government of the day had it made proposals on its own initiative. But a more compelling reason for the use of outside bodies was almost certainly that governments make few friends out of local

[2] Full details of this and all other Reports cited are in the Select Bibliography on p. 172.

government reform, and are certain to upset a number of local people, particularly those who stand to lose office and status from the creation of larger authorities. In any case, if a government proposes legislation on the basis of an independent expert report, it can claim to be following politically impartial advice.

Three further committees of inquiry examined the internal organization of local government. The Maud Committee on Management and its sister Committee on Staffing (under Sir George Mallaby's chairmanship) both sat for the three years 1964 to 1967. And in 1971 the Government established a study group, mainly of local-authority members and officers, to consider what management structures would best suit the new local councils to be created under the 1972 Local Government Act. A seven-man working party under the Clerk of Kent County Council, Mr. M. A. Bains, produced a report in 1972—'The New Local Authorities: Management and Structure'.

The reasons for creating this second group of committees were rather different. The internal organization of a local council is essentially a matter for that council itself. A government could enforce a particular organizational structure by legislation, but this no government would traditionally wish to do as it would blatantly offend against the principle that a democratically elected council should manage its own business. When such change is needed, therefore, it must be sought by co-operation and persuasion, and for this purpose the creation of committees by joint action between central and local government is an obviously sensible device. All three of these committees were appointed jointly by the Government and the national associations representing the different types of local authority; indeed, the Maud and Mallaby Committees were created on local government initiative.

Finally mention must also be made of two other committees of inquiry. The first, the Seebohm Committee on Local Authority and Allied Personal Social Services, produced a comprehensive set of proposals in 1968 after three years' work. It recommended a stronger local authority structure, with a single social services department for each council in place of the fragmented provision of services through two or three separate departments. The use of a committee here was clearly justified by the fact that a wide range of services had gradually been developed over the years by various kinds of local council and voluntary body under the supervision of several different departments of central government.

A second major functional inquiry was made in 1969 to 1971, into the future of water and sewage services, this time by a statutory permanent committee, the Central Advisory Water Committee. This proposed the creation of regional and area water authorities and the removal of water supply and sewage disposal functions from local government.

Compared with this long list of independent inquiries, there are only two important examples of a government undertaking its own review. A lengthy review of local government finance culminated in a set of proposals published in 1971. This rejected the possibility of any major new sources of local revenue either supplementing or replacing the only tax available at present to local councils, namely the rate. An equally prolonged study of the National Health Service led to two 'green' papers, issued as consultative documents by Labour and Conservative governments in turn, and finally in 1972 to a 'white' paper which proposed the establishment of regional and area health authorities and the removal from local authorities of their clinics, health centres, ambulances, nurses, and health visitors.

These several inquiries, whether internal or by an independent body, do not comprise a comprehensive list. Numerous others could be cited, including reviews of the public library service, transport and traffic, police, refuse collection and disposal, development plans and public participation in planning. But these latter ones had only minor influence on the structure and working of local government.

THE RESULTS

Besides taking decisions on its own reviews of the National Health Service and of local government finance, the Government had also to react to the many independent reports cited above. In theory it could treat their recommendations in any of four ways: ignore, reject, modify, or enact.

History gives many examples of a government taking one of the first two possible courses. Most commonly over the years, committee reports have been conveniently forgotten, more rarely they have been rejected. Neither fate befell any of the local government inquiries made in this period.

The functional reviews and the Government's internal review of finance all led to new legislation along the lines of the original proposals. In 1970, for example, the Local Authority Social Services Act closely followed the recommendations of the Seebohm Committee, and in 1973 two acts were passed reorganizing the National Health Service and the services concerned with water and sewage, both of which were based on the earlier inquiries.

The recommendations of the three committees which looked into the internal organization of local authorities did not, for the most part, call for legislation. What was chiefly needed here was local decision; but the Local Government Act of 1972 went part of the way towards meeting the criticism made by two of the reports that local councils were obliged by law to appoint too many specific chief officers and committees: it did away with a number of statutory appointments, though not for education, fire, police, and social services.

In view of the local controversy which always surrounds proposals for the amalgamation of local authorities, the outcome of the reviews of local government structure was still more surprising. The proposals of the various committees were not adopted as they stood, but they led directly to major Acts of Parliament in 1963 and 1972 which together recast the whole structure of English local government.

The origins of the 1963 London Government Act were firmly rooted in the 1960 Herbert Commission Report, and the notion of a new Greater London Council (G.L.C.) covering the 8,000,000 inhabitants of built-up London which was central to that report was at the centre of the act. The idea of an important second tier of London boroughs was also in both report and act, though the latter plumped for rather fewer (thirty-two) than the former (fifty-two).

At first sight the 1972 act followed much less closely from the Redcliffe-Maud Report of 1969. But here again it was the report that generated the momentum which led first the Labour Government and then the Conservative one that succeeded it to decide to introduce legislation. The act created a two-level system of local government throughout England (and Wales), whereas the report had favoured all-purpose authorities outside the conurbations.

The Local Government Boundary Commission, set up under the 1972 act as a permanent body with responsibility for keeping local authority areas up to date, produced a report on the boundaries of county districts which the Government implemented *in toto*; and, because of its ability to look impartially at local boundaries, the commission seems likely to have its future reports adopted. During debates on the 1972 act, the Government promised that it would operate a convention whereby proposals from the commission would normally be implemented without question. This is in marked contrast to the position in the early 1960s, when the Local Government Commission for England made several recommendations for boundary changes which the Government subsequently rejected—the *cause célèbre* being Rutland, by far the smallest English county, which launched a campaign to fight the proposed amalgamation with Leicestershire, and won.

Of all the reviews mentioned above, only one still remains under consideration. How will the Government handle the proposals of the Crowther–Kilbrandon Commission on the Constitution? Will this be as successful as its predecessors in leading to legislation, or will it be the one clear recent instance of a report ignored?

The basic structure of local government, found in the acts of 1888 and 1894, did not change much for more than three-quarters of a century. Certainly the two principles of democracy and the urban–rural dichotomy were central to official thinking up to 1966, when the Redcliffe-Maud Commission was given wide enough terms of reference to reconsider the second principle, if not the first. But this adherence to a basic structure did not prevent the actual system of local government from undergoing detailed change during the first half of the present century.

The most common alteration was in the functions allocated to local government. Decisions here were always piecemeal: a service added, a service taken away, or responsibility moved from the lower to the upper tier in counties. Financial changes also occurred from time to time: the rating system overhauled, the grants system amended. Nor did boundaries remain entirely static: during the period 1888 to 1926 there were changes in some county-borough, and during the 1930s in some district, boundaries. The Herbert and Redcliffe-Maud Commissions, however, were the first comprehensive investigations into the structure of English local government ever undertaken; nor were there precedents for such inquiries into the internal organization of local councils as those of the Maud and Mallaby Committees.

2

The Purpose of Local Government

ACCORDING to the Herbert Commission, the purpose of local government 'is to do for people what a group of persons, elected according to law by a majority of the citizens but on election becoming representative of them all, conceive to be good within the limit of their legal powers'.[1] In other words, there are two main facts about local government: it is a provider of services to a local community and an instrument of democratic self-government, not a mere agent of the national state.

A PROVIDER OF SERVICES *no longer*

Local government in modern England is the creation of Parliament. This was not always so; there were local governors of a sort long before Parliament came into being. But the organs of local government today take all their important characteristics from Acts of Parliament. Further, Parliament has not been content merely to give them powers and a set of bounds beyond which they may not pass: in some cases it has also positively prescribed what they must do. Local authorities are thus obliged to provide certain services and allowed to provide others. They can do practically nothing else which costs money (since 1963 a small amount has been expendable on anything they consider to be in the interests of the area or its inhabitants).

Thus English local government has no inherent right to be responsible for any particular service. Only Parliament can decide

[1] *Report of Royal Commission on Local Government in Greater London*, Cmnd. 1164 (H.M.S.O., 1960), para. 229.

what body is to be responsible for a public service, whether a central government department, an elected local authority, or some form of public corporation. And from time to time Parliament has changed its mind. The twentieth century is studded with examples of reallocated responsibility.

Changes in the functions of local government since the acts of 1888 and 1894 can be classified under five main headings:

(1) Traditional (i.e. Victorian or pre-Victorian) functions of local government transferred to central government or *ad hoc* agencies. Trunk roads (1936), hospitals (1946), valuation for rating (1948), and (from 1974) water supply and sewage-disposal services are examples.

(2) Traditional functions originally performed by *ad hoc* local bodies but later taken over by general purpose local authorities. A major aim of the 1888 and 1894 acts was to reduce the number of separate bodies providing a single service, and although for this purpose the acts themselves had only limited success, subsequent legislation led to the abolition of school boards (1902) and Poor Law unions (1929), with local authorities taking over their services.

(3) New (i.e. post-Victorian) functions given to local authorities and remaining their responsibility. Examples are housing, town and country planning (1909), the creation of smokeless zones (1956), and many of the social services, such as those for the aged and handicapped, which existed only in a rudimentary form until recent years.

(4) New functions given to local authorities and subsequently transferred to the central government or some *ad hoc* agency created by the Government. Clinics, maternity, and family planning services, for instance, were developed within local government but since 1974 come under the control of the new regional and area health authorities.

(5) Functions for which responsibility has been reallocated within the structure of local government. On the whole this has been a one-way process, upwards from the smaller to the larger area: in the period 1944–8 a number of services (town planning, personal health and welfare, elementary education, fire protection, for example) were taken away from district councils and given to county councils. Only in London and six other large conurbations has there been a marked devolution downwards. In these metropolitan areas the 1963 and 1972 acts allocated

responsibility for public libraries, education (though not in inner London), and the social services to district councils, whereas most of these had previously been the responsibility of county councils for many years.

These examples illustrate the large number of changes which have occurred in the work done by local authorities. Sometimes a change has been necessary because local councils have found increasing difficulty in coping with a service owing to the constraints put on them by their size—trunk roads, for example, outgrew local government and became a national responsibility with the increasing number of cars and lorries. Other changes have been made on grounds of national policy: in 1974, for example, the personal health services were removed from local authority control partly because the Government could apply its principle of amalgamating the several parts of the National Health Service only by the expedient of creating a series of appointed bodies and thus gaining the support of doctors who would not have been ready to serve under elected local councils.

What, then, are the major services provided by local authorities today? Because of their number (more than forty were listed in 1966 in evidence to the Redcliffe-Maud Commission), the answer to this question calls for some kind of classification. Three labels which seem useful are Protection, Welfare, and Convenience. Protection covers such services as police and fire prevention, while the building of roads and (in some areas) provision of buses are good examples of Convenience services. Much less easy to define are Welfare services, and here a series of subclassifications may be helpful. Some of these services are concerned directly with the welfare of man himself (either because of his age or his circumstances), while others are concerned primarily with his environment (either by positive provision or by the prevention or removal of unpleasant features of it). The distinction between these headings is not always easy to make—should housing, for example, come under Welfare or Convenience? Recreation raises the same question. The classification has at least the advantage that it can be expressed diagramatically (see Table 1).

Protection

Keeping the peace is the oldest form of service provided by government and responsibility for a police force has been a local government function for a very long time. London has long been excep-

TABLE 1 : *Local government services*

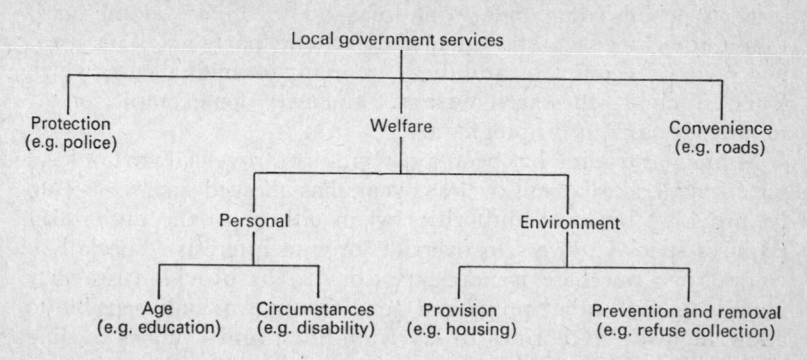

tional: in the square mile of the city itself there is still a police force for which the city corporation is responsible, but for the rest of the metropolitan area central, not local, government has direct police responsibility, exercised through the Metropolitan Police Commissioner, the Home Office, and the Home Secretary.

Other Protective services provided by local authorities include fire and civil defence, though the latter has dwindled in importance over recent years. Consumer protection, on the other hand, has been a developing service, and many local councils have built up large organizations (sometimes known as trading standards departments) in efforts to ensure that shoppers have fair treatment.

Convenience

Roads and bridges along with associated traffic controls such as parking places and speed limits, are of outstanding importance under this heading, not simply in their own right but because they are the one Convenience service that *must* be provided by local authorities. Indeed, in rural areas roads and bridges, together with cemeteries, allotments, and smallholdings (all of which must be provided if there is a demand), may be all that are provided.

In many towns, however, authorities have gone well beyond this basic range of Convenience services. These councils have developed a series of services commonly called municipal trading enterprises. Many run their own bus service, some own civic restaurants and entertainment centres (theatres and piers, for example). Markets and slaughter-houses are frequently owned by the local authority, as are more than a score of our airports (including those at Liverpool, Manchester, and Birmingham, but not Prestwick or the London airports, which come under a national body). Finally, some maritime authorities own and operate docks and harbours. This list is not, of course, complete, and there are many individual cases which could be cited—the race-course at Doncaster, for example, or the municipal bank in Birmingham.

Municipal trading has been a specially controversial part of local government. Parliament over the years has allowed such services to be provided by local authorities when either (a) the undertaker requires special powers to override private interests (especially if compulsory purchase is necessary), or (b) its provision is closely bound up with other municipal activities (it was only sensible to allow highway authorities to lay tram-lines, and councils owning piers to provide amenities on them), or (c) it can only be run as a monopoly, and the local authority can protect citizens from abuses which they might suffer from a private monopolist, or (d) private enterprise was not interested because it could not make a profit.

This leaves many important borderline cases which have been the chief subjects of controversy. These are of two kinds. First, over such things as restaurants, theatres, or other forms of entertainment the question may arise whether it is equitable for a local council, backed by the financial resources of the community, to compete with private enterprise and individual rate-payers.

The second type of controversy arises over the question who should provide a service about which there is general agreement that it should be publicly owned. Gas, electricity, and water illustrate the problem. On the one hand it is argued that each service needs to be administered over areas defined by reference to its own geographic or technical nature (the course of a river, for example, and its catchment area), and that national administration enables advantage to be taken of economies of scale, allows resources to be more easily moved between areas, and leads to the equitable spread of costs between consumers, regardless of where they live. Against this it is often claimed that unless a service is the responsibility of an elected local authority, neither will it be responsive to democratic control nor properly integrated with kindred local services and, further, that small-scale enterprises are more sensitive to the local situation and can be run more economically. Three times since the war this dispute has been brought to a head, and each time the Government and Parliament have favoured national ownership. In 1948 all gas and electricity under-takings were nationalized, as were the water-based services in 1974.

Welfare: Personal Services

Most of the services classified in this chapter under the Welfare heading have developed in the twentieth century. These are the growth services of local government. The local authority of Victorian times, with its emphasis on protection and convenience, had a very different image from the authority of the 1970s.

The personal services in particular are creatures of this century. As Table 1 indicated, they can be divided into two types: those provided because of the age of the recipient and those provided because of his or her circumstances.

(1) *Age*. It used to be said of local authorities that they were involved 'from womb to tomb'. The reorganization of the National Health Service in 1974 makes this statement less true today than formerly, for the provision of clinics, midwives, and home nurses has been taken over by the new regional and area health authorities. Though a local council may still provide a home help to assist with housework for a while each side of childbirth, its involvement in the first few months of a child's life is now small.

Until a child goes to school at the age of five local authority services affect its development in two main, related ways. First, there are play-groups and day nurseries. Secondly, some local education authorities maintain nursery schools. Both these services have been expanding rapidly in recent years, and it is now esti-mated that by 1981 some 90 per cent of four-year-olds and 50 per cent of three-year-olds will be receiving part-time nursery education.

The education service dominates local government in terms both of its financial importance and of its number of employees, account-ing for about half the local government total in each case. The great majority of children aged five to sixteen (for whom education is compulsory) attend schools maintained by the local education authority (the county, metropolitan district, or London borough council—and the Inner London Education Authority (I.L.E.A.) in the twelve central London boroughs), though some continue to attend private fee-paying schools or direct-grant grammar schools which receive a grant direct from the department of education and science. At local authority schools a number of ancillary services are also provided, notably dinners and school milk.

Local education authorities provide further services for young people over the age of sixteen and adults of any age who wish to continue with their studies. Many stay on at school until eighteen or nineteen and study for advanced level examinations. Others go to technical colleges and colleges of further education, either to sit similar examinations or to take vocational courses. Finally, local authorities in various parts of the country are responsible for the thirty polytechnics at which the emphasis is on degree courses. They also give grants to students who go on to universities, though here they act primarily as an agent of central government and have little discretion in the amount of the grant awarded.

A further group of age-based services is made available for retired people. Such services vary from area to area but frequently include luncheon clubs, cheap bus tickets, and old people's homes. Many senior citizens make no use of these services which, although age-based, could fall appropriately enough under the heading of circumstances-based.

(2) *Circumstances.* Local authority social service departments, in county and metropolitan districts, are providing more and more services for citizens suffering from difficult personal circumstances. The blind and deaf, the disabled, the physically and mentally handicapped, are all entitled to receive help, whether through home visits by trained social workers or in residential homes, training centres, or workshops. In almost every area council activity is supplemented by the work of voluntary organizations; the sensible local authority works closely with such bodies, frequently by providing money to help pay for their overheads.

Helping children in various kinds of need is also a function of social service departments. Foster parents or adopters may be found; children's homes are provided and, since 1963, money can be spent in order to keep families together and so prevent a child from coming into the care of a local council (for example, a grant towards a rent or gas bill may be made to prevent an eviction or loss of comfort). The local education department is also concerned with handicapped children who require special education: in 1970 over 85,000 were attending 986 special schools up and down the country, and 90 per cent of such schools were maintained by local education authorities.

Welfare: Environmental Services
In broad terms, the task of the local authority here is to enhance the quality of life in its area. It seeks to do this by providing certain

services and by preventing or removing things which would or do spoil the environment.

(1) *Provision.* Providing clean water was a traditional function of local government, but since 1974 it has passed on to the new regional water authorities. Town and country planning, the enforcement of building regulations, and the provision of housing now become the major tasks under this head. Neither planning nor building regulations directly provide anything but both are concerned to ensure that what others provide is good. Planners decide on the future pattern of the use to be made of land in their area. The building regulations set standards for builders of houses and other developers and provide for adequate ventilation and light in all buildings. Since 1965 there have been national building regulations which local authorities enforce; previously each council operated its own building by-laws and not all of these have been repealed.

The provision of leisure facilities is growing apace in many parts of the country. Swimming-baths and sports facilities, arts centres and theatres have recently been developed in growing numbers, and local councils have been reclaiming places such as disused railways and canals for use as hiking and picnic areas. The traditional town park and set of football pitches are but one aspect of a developing service for recreation and leisure.[2]

Local housing authorities have a general responsibility to consider the housing conditions and needs of their area. There are several ways in which they can act. Traditionally the most important has been through the construction of houses and flats to rent: in 1973 one house in four was owned by a local council and over 4,000,000 families had a municipal landlord. The council allocates tenancies and maintains its properties in a good state of repair. Until the Housing Finance Act of 1972 it also had a considerable amount of discretion as to the level of rents to be charged. Now a 'fair rent' is fixed for each property and has to be approved by a national appointed board.

Other ways in which housing authorities frequently act are through selling council houses to their occupants (a policy which is frequently the subject of dispute between the local political parties), lending money to citizens seeking to purchase a house, and supporting the activities of non-profit-making housing associations.

---

[2] In 1973 a select committee of the House of Lords made several recommendations for further developments in the sporting and leisure fields.

Finally, slum clearance and environmental improvement are more appropriately considered under the next heading.

(2) *Prevention and Removal*. An important list of services provided by local authorities can be drawn up under this heading. The regular removal of refuse, the control of smoke through the declaration of 'smokeless zones', and controls over persons carrying out 'offensive trades' (such as glue-makers and rag- or bone-dealers) are examples. Since 1974 responsibility for the disposal of sewage has been shared with the regional and area water authorities.

Great emphasis is now placed on the improvement of the environment and local government is making an increasingly important contribution in several ways. The reclamation of derelict land, declaration of conservation areas (to preserve our architectural heritage), and cleaning of old buildings are three examples. Slum clearance and the provision of general improvement areas are others. Under the former the council purchases and demolishes housing which lacks basic amenities of water, light, or heat or which is damp or likely to fall down. Other residential areas where the houses are better constructed may be rehabilitated as general improvement areas: here the council gives grants to owners to assist with repairs and modernization and itself provides general amenities such as play areas and parking spaces.

This completes a preliminary view of the welfare services which together constitute perhaps the most important part of modern English local government. Two points of general interest are worth emphasizing. First, local authorities have sole responsibility for very few of these services. In education, housing, and the social services the local authority is only one worker among others. Private enterprise, voluntary bodies, and the central government also have their significant parts to play.

Secondly, these services are not provided uniformly throughout England. One of the principal reasons for local government is the variety of circumstances to be found in different parts of the country. Slum clearance, for example, is less important in newly developed areas than in old industrial towns. Local initiative varies: local politicians vary in their conception of the level of services that should be provided, and voluntary workers are far more active in some areas than in others. This general account therefore of the work done by local government should not be taken to imply that all these services are available over the whole of England, still less that a similar standard of service is offered by all authorities.

Between the minimum of services which must be provided and the maximum which a council may not exceed, there is a wide area of discretion.

A DEMOCRATIC INSTITUTION

It is in the exercise of this discretion that the second purpose of local government becomes apparent. A distinction can be made between the provision of services and their *effective* provision—that is, to the satisfaction of the consumer—and it is to secure the latter that the local government system has a democratic base.

The generally accepted importance of this democratic base was reflected clearly in the terms of reference of the two major royal commissions mentioned in the previous chapter. The Herbert Commission was instructed to consider whether any changes in the metropolitan area 'would better secure effective and convenient local government'. The Redcliffe-Maud Commission, in blunter language, was told to take into account 'the need to sustain a viable system of local democracy'. Although neither commission was specifically barred from making recommendations which would have converted any part of local government into local administration by civil servants accountable to Whitehall and Westminster, such proposals would have been inconsistent with the spirit of their terms of reference.

To many people local democracy implies little more than the periodic exercise of the right to vote at elections of local councillors. Indeed the majority of those entitled to vote do not even participate in local affairs to this small extent, as the local election figures show. Elections are undoubtedly an essential element of democracy and give citizens the chance to pass judgement on the past actions of a government and on its future credibility. But the concept of local democracy goes well beyond mere attendance at the polling station and includes such ideas as accountability and control, responsiveness, and the redress of grievance.

Accountability and control

A clear distinction between local government and local administration is that local councils are directly accountable for their actions whereas local administrations are not. The latter, which include gas and electricity boards, health and water authorities, and decentralized post office and social security services, are controlled only from above through the activities of Parliament, ministers, and the courts of law. Local governments are also accountable to Parliament and the courts, a subject which will be explored in Chapters 9 and 10. But in addition local councillors have to face their electorates every four years. The local election ensures a measure of local accountability.

Often even this control seems at first sight more apparent than real. Elections to the majority of English local authorities are conducted on party lines, with two consequences. First, in many areas it is rare for political control to change hands: some authorities have been controlled by the same party since before the second world war, and many others have been dominated by one party with only an occasional and temporary change. Secondly, local election results seem to depend more on the national standing of the parties than on local factors. Despite this, local elections are a valid method of emphasizing accountability and control. Councillors know that they have to face re-election in the future, and they are likely to take this into account when faced with difficult policy choices. They can never be certain that their future is assured: the national average figures conceal numerous local election upsets. And party support is necessary in order to obtain nomination. Thus it can be argued that, indirectly, the election is effective in persuading councillors to *anticipate* the likely local reaction to alternative decisions.

Responsiveness

This is not something which can be easily measured. The argument about anticipated reactions suggests that councillors are responsive to local pressures. It is certainly true that there is a far greater coverage of local government than of local administrations in the mass media. Most areas of England are well served by local newspapers and many by local radio stations, all of which devote a great deal of attention to local government affairs. By contrast, the meetings of health or water authorities receive scant publicity. Indeed, Parliament was sufficiently conscious of this to establish local advisory councils under the Water Act of 1973 to give 'direct expression of the public's views'. But such bodies, like their counterparts in the post office, transport, gas, and electricity fields, are appointed rather than elected and remain quite anonymous. Few consumers of these services know of their existence.

It is through the activities of the local press and of local pressure groups, and because councillors and local government officers are anxious to preserve their local reputations, that local government obtains a sensitivity which is peculiar to it. Whenever a controversial matter requires decision a council will test the local climate of opinion before taking action and will have in mind the consequences of taking an unpopular line.

Redress of Grievance

This concept specially concerns an individual's relations with his local authority. Further, it is possible to distinguish decisions which have been implemented from those which are (or are not) being contemplated, and whereas accountability and responsiveness are largely related to the latter, the redress of grievance concerns the former type of case.

Traditionally it is the councillor who has been responsible for investigating or taking up complaints about local services. Until 1974 local government had no special machinery of its own—the councillor apart—for handling complaints about its services. One exception to this general statement covered complaints against the police: a senior officer may be appointed to investigate such allegations. Another was a move by one or two local authorities (notably Bristol) in the mid-1960s to establish a local 'office of complaints', but this idea was not followed up in other areas. In 1974 there was a major new development in the establishment of regional Commissioners (or 'ombudsmen') with powers to look into complaints from citizens of local authority maladministration.

Until the creation of the ombudsmen in 1974 it had normally been assumed that local authorities were themselves capable of handling complaints. The sensitive nature of local government, compared with locally appointed bodies, together with the accessibility of local councillors and officials, was usually taken to indicate that it is in the interests of a council to handle grievances quickly and effectively. But against this it can be argued that the councillor is, for two reasons, in a difficult position when pressed by a local resident to pursue a complaint on his behalf. First, he has constitutionally (if not actually) taken the decision of which complaint is made—unlike a Member of Parliament, who can claim that responsibility lies not with him but with the minister. The separation of executive and legislative powers which operates at the central government level is not found in the local government constitution. Secondly, to be effective in his council work a councillor needs to develop a working relationship with the professional officers. Such a relationship could be jeopardized by a councillor pressing complaints with too much zeal. In future many a councillor may find value in his ability to refer a matter to the local ombudsman for further investigation. So, too, may the citizen.

Local government in England, then, is more than a mere service-providing agency. It differs fundamentally, for example, from the administration of social security benefits. Local authorities have wide discretion over what they provide. The local social security officer has hardly any and works from a detailed rule-book provided by his parent ministry in London.[3]

It is the exercise of this local discretion which binds together the two essential features of local government: its functional and its democratic strands. The two are inextricably intertwined, and the health of local government depends on both. A duty to provide services without the sensitivity caused by the presence of local democracy is local administration, not local government. The existence of an elected local authority with insufficient powers and unable to be functionally effective as a result is not local government either, for it cannot 'govern'.

[3] There are in fact a few instances where local councils do act as agents of central departments—in maintaining trunk roads for example—but these are sharply distinguished from local government functions.

3

Reviews of the Old Structure

THE local government map today is quite different from that of the early 1960s. The London Government Act of 1963 and the Local Government Act of 1972 together redrew the map and reorganized the work of local authorities in every part of the country. This chapter discusses the background to these two acts, and Chapter 4 the new structure of local government that they produced.

The 1963 and 1972 acts were Parliament's response to the reports of the Herbert Commission on Local Government in Greater London[1] and of the Redcliffe-Maud Commission on Local Government in England.[2] The establishment of these two commissions followed years of growing dissatisfaction with the old structure of local government. There was fairly general agreement that it suffered from the following major weaknesses:

(1) Smallness—too many authorities lacked sufficient resources to be able to provide a wide range and high standard of services.

(2) Geography—the boundaries of most authorities, particularly of the larger towns, were out of date. Suburbs often lay outside the boundaries of a borough, and in parts of the country relations between big cities and the surrounding county areas had steadily deteriorated as arguments developed about such things as boundary extensions and the siting of 'overspill' housing.

(3) Complexity—there were no fewer than nine different types of elected local authority. Outside the larger towns some services were run by the county council and some by district councils. In addition, many county councils subdivided their area for the administration of some services or used county district councils to

---

[1] Cmnd. 1164 (1960).   [2] Cmnd. 4040 (1969).

run certain services under schemes of delegation. It was therefore extremely difficult to know who was responsible for what.

(4) Apathy—many observers deplored the low turn-out figures at local elections, and the apparent lack of either interest or knowledge among the bulk of the population.

(5) Subordination—local authorities were too dependent on central government for funds, and subject to too many instructions.

Two facts had also become apparent. Piecemeal alteration to particular areas could not hope to achieve a reorganization sufficiently far-reaching to have an impact on these five weaknesses. Secondly, though the several associations of existing local authorities had gradually come to agree that reform was necessary, they were far from agreement on what that reform should be. Wide-ranging independent inquiry was therefore needed if a new structure was to be found, and such inquiries the two royal commissions were to carry out. They were asked to consider the hotch-potch of local authorities and recommend a structure of local government which would be both functionally and democratically viable. These points will be discussed in turn.

THE OLD STRUCTURE: A HOTCH-POTCH

How was the map of England divided in, say, 1961, the year of the last decennial census before the establishment of the new structure of local government in Greater London? The short answer is 'according to the principle, laid down in the 1888 Local Government Act, that towns should be governed separately from the rural areas which surround them'. This means that from a map of England there should first be abstracted the wholly urbanized county of London. This administrative county (that of the London County Council or L.C.C.) covered roughly speaking those parts of the metropolis within a five- or six-mile radius of the centre, where by 1961 there were living some $3\frac{1}{4}$ million people, a figure which had steadily fallen for several decades as those whose means enabled them to move their homes out of town did so. The L.C.C. area was subdivided into twenty-nine parts: twenty-eight metropolitan boroughs and the corporation of the City of London shared the provision of services with the L.C.C.

From the rest of the map, seventy-nine more holes now have to be cut. These were large cities and towns which had the status of both a borough and a county and were therefore called county boroughs. They ran all local government services in their area and for this reason were commonly described as all-purpose local authorities. Some were very large: Birmingham contained more than a million people, while Liverpool, Manchester, and Sheffield had populations of more than half a million. Others were much smaller, and thirty-three contained fewer than 100,000 inhabitants. More than 13,000,000 people, or almost exactly 30 per cent of the population of England, lived in these county boroughs.

The map now looks the worse for wear, with holes almost everywhere, particularly in the more urbanized parts of the country. The geographical county of Lancashire contained as many as seventeen county boroughs, while large parts of West Yorkshire and the Black Country around Birmingham were also under county borough government. But it is this remnant of the map of England which was divided into forty-eight irregular patches called administrative counties. Again they varied in size, in terms both of population and of area. The administrative county of Lancashire contained 2·2 million people (despite the abstraction of the seventeen holes within it), almost a hundred times the population of Rutland. Devon's 1,650,000 acres could be contrasted with the 53,000 of the county of Soke of Peterborough. Many of these counties had boundaries which could be traced back to medieval times or even earlier.

Unlike the county boroughs, administrative counties were not all-purpose local authorities. The county council elected in each of them shared the provision of services with separately elected councils covering sub-areas of the county. These can collectively be called 'county districts', though there were, in fact, three different types. As with the distinction between county and county borough, the division of a county into districts was based on the concept of the small town having its own local authority, separate from the authority for the rural areas round it. Many older towns had obtained charters and were called municipal boroughs. Other towns were urban districts. Groups of villages formed rural districts, and within a rural district each village had a parish council or, in the case of very small villages, a regular parish meeting at which any resident had the right to speak his mind.

This was the structure on which the local government of England rested (see Table 2). As the figures in brackets show, in 1961 there were more than 1,300 directly elected local authorities in England (excluding the 10,000 parishes, for in practice parish meetings and councils were not responsible for any major local government service). This large number meant that many of them were very

TABLE 2. *The structure of local government, 1961*

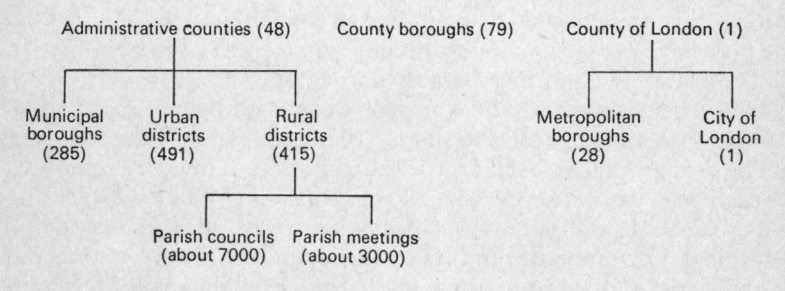

Figures in brackets represent the number of authorities in 1961

small in population and resources. Of the 1,191 county districts (i.e. municipal boroughs, urban and rural districts) only 469 contained as many as 20,000 inhabitants. Seventeen county boroughs and three administrative counties were below 75,000 population— yet they were responsible for important services like education, town and country planning, and the welfare and children's services. Such work calls for the employment of highly qualified and expensive staff, and this cannot be justified in services provided for minority groups such as the blind, the deaf, or the mentally handicapped except in areas wide enough to provide sufficient 'case-loads'.

The second major criticism of the old structure was that it contained too many geographical anomalies. There were those who held the view that the traditional distinction between town and country had become increasingly unreal as personal mobility became the norm rather than the exception following the development of motor transport. A town might have been commercially and socially distinct from near-by villages at the time of the 1888 act, it was argued, but this was no longer true if account was taken of patterns such as the journey to work. Nor could older towns solve their housing problems without co-operation from surrounding areas for they lacked land in the town.

This argument of principle was largely put forward by academics and had little support from either local or central government until quite recently. The Herbert Commission, for example, was charged in its terms of reference with the task of studying an area only a little larger than that of the Metropolitan Police District. It reported that 'the influence of London extends far beyond the Review Area'[3] and that in choosing the review area the Government intended only 'to include the main built-up area of London'.[4]

A year after the appointment of the Herbert Commission a body called the Local Government Commission for England was established under the provisions of the 1958 Local Government Act. This commission was to review provincial local authority boundaries, and here again official thinking still favoured the town–country dichotomy. The commission could propose the extension of the boundaries of county boroughs; but its terms of reference (and its interpretation of them) meant that only those suburbs of a town which were continuously urbanized were considered for inclusion in the borough. It could propose the creation of new counties in the provincial conurbations, but these conurbations (called 'special review areas') were defined in terms only of the continuously built-up area. Until the Redcliffe-Maud Commission was set up in 1966 with wider terms of reference, official thinking remained firmly attached to the principle of separate governing bodies for town and country.

There were those who attacked the geography of local government in terms of its practical anomalies rather than its underlying principles. Almost any county borough, certainly any which had grown in recent decades, was fairly sure to have a boundary which ran through the built-up area of its post-1930 suburbs. This was simply because it had been almost impossible to obtain boundary extensions to match physical development following Acts of Parliament passed in 1926 and 1929. The creation of new county boroughs had also been virtually banned by these acts, and municipal boroughs like Cambridge, Ealing, and Luton had grown so rapidly since then that by 1961 they were far larger than a number of county boroughs. One could tidy up the system either by 'promoting' these towns to county boroughs, or by 'demoting' small county boroughs, or both. This, indeed, was a further part of the task given to the 1958 Local Government Commission.

This commission was made to follow a tortuous and lengthy

[3] Cmnd. 1164, para. 896.   [4] Ibid, para. 902.

procedure before making final recommendations for an area. It issued a detailed questionnaire to all authorities in the area and held informal consultations with them before publishing draft proposals. Local authorities, and anyone else who was interested, could send the commission written representations on these, and this was followed by a statutory conference to discuss the draft proposals. Finally, the commission reported to the Minister, who then had to hold a public inquiry into objections to the report before making a decision. This process was both time-consuming and repetitive. Every local authority had so many opportunities to protest against any proposed change that would-be reformers had to sustain their case over several years. The commission took from twenty-nine to fifty-four months to issue a report: ministers frequently took even longer to implement, modify, or reject it.[5]

In addition to procedural difficulties, the politics of reform made change unlikely. Extensions to county boroughs or the creation of new ones were bitterly opposed by county and district councils threatened with the loss of territory.[6] The demotion of a county borough could not be undertaken lightly, as this meant that the town would no longer be responsible for several major services—education, local health and welfare services, the children's service, town and country planning, the police and fire services being the main ones which would be taken over by the county. No small county wanted to amalgamate—because such a merger would usually be with a much larger neighbour.

Despite these heavy odds, some changes were made during the seven years of the commission's labour. Luton, Torbay, and Solihull became county boroughs; four counties were merged into two in the Cambridgeshire–Huntingdonshire area; and the boundaries of twenty-five county boroughs were rationalized through extensions, including five in the Black Country, where the conurbation centred on Birmingham became almost wholly covered by county boroughs. But there were failures too. No county borough was demoted, despite several recommendations from the commission; the plan for a new urban county for Tyneside was not accepted; and the smallest county (Rutland) persuaded the Government that amalgamation with neighbouring Leicestershire was unnecessary. However, the commission's very lack of success proved valuable, for it illus-

[5] H. V. Wiseman (ed.), *Local Government in England 1958–69* (Routledge & Kegan Paul, 1970), Ch. 2.

[6] It was a series of such fights that had led earlier to the 1926 and 1929 acts.

trated the need for a different and more radical approach if local government was to be successfully reformed. It helped to persuade the Government to appoint the Redcliffe-Maud Commission in 1966.

Reference should also be made at this point to the third major weakness of the old structure—the complexity of administrative arrangements. The map of English local government which has on it no more than the boundaries of the authorities included in Table 2 (p. 26 above) tells only part of the story. The actual administration of many important local government services was being conducted over quite different areas.

Some services were being provided jointly by two or more authorities, to meet the argument that individual authorities were too small. In 1961 some half a dozen county boroughs did not have their own police force but formed part of the neighbouring county for police purposes. Virtually every county borough fell into this category by the end of the decade, following compulsory amalgamations of police forces after 1966 by the Home Secretary under the terms of the Police Act of 1964. Joint fire and ambulance services along similar lines were not unknown, and joint water boards with several county districts represented on them (water supply was a county district service in areas outside London where there was no private water company) also became common during the 1960s following government policy decisions.

On the other hand some county council services were administered on the principle of devolution. The geographical size of many counties made this administratively sensible: it would be ridiculous to base all child care officers at county hall in, say, Preston or Exeter, when they would sometimes be dealing with cases more than 30 miles away. In such services efficiency alone demanded some deconcentration, for the sake of both staff and client.

For the welfare, children's, community health, local planning, and education services, however, devolution frequently meant more than the mere establishment of a 'local county hall'. It included the concept of the area, or 'divisional', committee on which would serve both county and district councillors. Such a committee would control the day-to-day administration of many aspects of these services, within the limits of county policy. A division normally covered the area of two or more county districts, but the larger municipal boroughs and urban districts (with a population in excess of 60,000) could often claim as of right to be 'excepted districts' and have a separate divisional committee of their own —which was, in effect, a committee of the borough or district council.

This additional layer of government was largely a relic of history. Until the period 1944–8 many district councils had been responsible for parts of the education, local health and welfare, and children's services. Districts had also been responsible for the development of town planning. In transferring responsibility for these services wholly to the county councils the government of the day met severe opposition from the districts, in particular the larger ones. The 1944 Education Act incorporated the concept of area committees in order to offer districts some continued involvement in the service. Divisional executives for education became normal in most counties, as did area committees for the other services following later legislation.

This added layer made the local government map even more complicated, especially in the many counties where the several departments of a county council did not choose the same pattern of divisions. Cheshire County Council, for instance, told the Local Government Commission for England in 1962 that for education it had fifteen divisional executives and two area subcommittees; fifteen area committees for health (only ten of which were coterminous with the education areas); seven for welfare; five for the children's service; and seven area offices (but no area committees) for controlling development of land-use (coterminous with the welfare areas). For a resident of Stalybridge, this meant area offices in Dukinfield for education, in Stalybridge for health, in Wilmslow for children, and in Stockport for planning, while for welfare there was no administration at area level.

A final point about devolution to excepted districts and area committees was that this did not always improve relations between county councils and their districts. Where there were no clashes of policy, the system operated smoothly enough. But in some counties policy disputes were not infrequent—sometimes because parts of a county were under different political control from the county council, sometimes because larger district councils were anxious to demonstrate that they would be effective as county boroughs if they could obtain the necessary 'promotion'. This latter motive was particularly noticeable in the outer area of Greater London where several district councils in Essex and Middlesex were larger than many provincial county boroughs. The tension between county and districts which resulted led the Herbert Commission to conclude that 'where (tension) exists in acute form, as in Middlesex, it makes successful local government almost impossible'.[7]

THE SEARCH FOR FUNCTIONAL EFFECTIVENESS

This, then, was the situation which faced both the Herbert and the Redcliffe-Maud Commissions. A highly fragmented structure of local government was further weakened by internal friction: battles between municipal and county authorities over the creation of new and extensions of existing county boroughs; disputes between county and district councils over the running of certain services; an apparent lack of public enthusiasm for local government; and an undesirably large amount of central control over the work of local councils.

In the face of this both commissions saw their task as one of seeking a quite new structure of local government which would be both functionally and democratically viable. 'In examining our problem we have tried always to keep simultaneously in mind these two twin matters, administrative efficiency and the health of representative government, as well as the organic relationship of both', stated the Herbert Commission.[8] Nine years later, the Redcliffe-Maud Commission drew attention to the phrase 'the need to sustain a viable system of local democracy' in its terms of reference. 'This we take to be of importance at least equal to the importance of securing efficiency in the provision of services', said the report.[9]

For a local authority to be an efficient provider of services, apart from other considerations must it have at least a minimum population? Does this figure vary from one service to another? All dispassionate observers were agreed that small counties and county boroughs with populations of only 50,000 or 60,000 were too small to be able to provide a full education service. Most also felt that tiny district councils serving only 4,000 or 5,000 people were too small for housing and public health functions. Diagnosis of the problem was not too difficult; reaching a generally agreed solution proved to be very difficult indeed.

The Herbert Commission was particularly restricted in its choice of options for two reasons. First, it had insufficient resources to enable it to undertake much in the way of research of its own, whereas the Redcliffe-Maud Commission was able to sponsor a

[7] Cmnd. 1164, para, 680.   [8] Cmnd. 1164, para. 221.
[9] Cmnd. 4040, para. 28.

number of studies into the relationship between the size of an authority and its performance. Secondly, it was created at a time when the conventional view was that a town of 100,000 (or 125,000 in a conurbation) should be assumed to be large enough to function effectively as a county borough. This was the conclusion of the Government in the White Paper which preceded the 1958 Local Government Act, but it was not a conclusion based on objective study. The White Paper simply reflected a political agreement between the County Councils Association (C.C.A.) and the Association of Municipal Corporations (A.M.C.).[10]

Inevitably the Herbert Commission was influenced by this conventional wisdom, particularly when it was translated into law under the 1958 act, which established the Local Government Commission for England. If this was to be the normal minimum population level for an all-purpose county borough, why should the commission depart from it in London?

The report of the commission clearly reflected these two restrictions. It recommended the creation of a new council for Greater London, covering an area of around 15 miles radius from the centre and a population of about 8,000,000. Beneath this would be a series of fifty-two London boroughs. These would be responsible for most local government services and would have populations of between 100,000 and 250,000. Existing boroughs of over 130,000 were not recommended for amalgamation, except two which adjoined small boroughs too small to continue on their own.

The commission's contribution to the debate about the minimum size for a local authority can be stated as follows. First, population alone is not a sufficient criterion. Certain services need to be run by authorities covering a particular *area* rather than population. Planning and transportation were clear examples of this. So too were ambulances, fire brigades, and main sewerage services. The minimum needs of these services were for an authority for the whole of Greater London and the figures of 100,000 or 125,000 generally thought appropriate for county borough status were far too low to be relevant. This approach did not entirely conflict with conventional wisdom in that the 1958 act gave the Local Government Commission the power to recommend the creation of conurbation-wide counties around Birmingham, Manchester, and some other large provincial centres.

[10] Ministry of Housing and Local Government, *Areas and Status of Local Authorities in England and Wales, Cmd 9831* (H.M.S.O., 1956), paras. 29–30.

Secondly, the commission rejected suggestions that the minimum size of a London borough should be a 200,000 population. This size had been mentioned to it 'more frequently than any other'; but none of the suggestions made to it could 'be regarded as scientific'. Also (a direct response to the 1956 White Paper agreement) 'a borough of 200,000 is a large authority by the standards of this country and there are authorities of half that size which no one could characterize as being inadequate for their responsibilities'.[11]

Thirdly, the commission concluded that the education service posed particular problems in London. Its proposed boroughs would be the main units of local government and would be responsible for most of the services provided by provincial county boroughs (apart from those mentioned above, where size of area was crucial). Logically the commission should have made the boroughs the local education authorities, given their population size of 100,000 plus. This would have meant creating fifty-two education authorities in place of nine—as was being proposed for the welfare and children's services. But the L.C.C. had paid no heed to metropolitan borough boundaries when developing its education system, and the fragmentation of its service would lead to problems of two kinds. Many more schoolchildren than was usual would have to be educated in schools of a neighbouring authority. And some education authorities would lack any further education facilities. Because of these acute difficulties, the commission proposed an exceptional arrangement. The new G.L.C. should be responsible for maintaining the general standard of education over the whole new area and should finance the service, while the boroughs should actually build and administer the schools and colleges.

The commission's views on the size of a local authority were accepted by the Government and by Parliament so far as the creation of a Greater London Council was concerned, but were amended in respect of the boroughs. The Government decided to increase the minimum population size of the boroughs to around 150,000, with an average of 250,000. A main purpose here was to overcome the education problem and make the boroughs full education authorities in their own right. Even so, it still proved difficult to dismantle and parcel out among the new boroughs the L.C.C. education service (because of tremendous political opposition, as well as for technical and administrative reasons), and a

[11] Cmnd. 1164, para. 926.

special body, the Inner London Education Authority (I.L.E.A.), was established to run the service in the inner area formerly covered by the L.C.C.

The establishment of the Redcliffe-Maud Commission in 1966 reopened the debate about the minimum size of a local authority. This time there was little prevailing conventional wisdom. It was too early to appraise the working of the new structure in London (established only in 1965), and few were happy with the provisions of the 1958 act or the progress made by the Local Government Commission. Further, the new royal commission was encouraged by the Government to spend money on research and to make whatever recommendations it might choose. It was given the widest possible terms of reference and when announcing its establishment Mr. Crossman, the Minister of Housing and Local Government, described the existing structure of local government as archaic, with far too many authorities functioning over inadequate areas.

There was an immediate response to the new climate of opinion. The commission quickly decided to undertake special research into the possible relationship between size and functional effectiveness. The findings tended to be inconclusive. Various government departments gave evidence which was often quite different from that which would have been offered a few years earlier, chiefly because they now favoured larger areas. The Department of Education and Science, for example, now indicated that 500,000 was a desirable minimum population for an education authority, implying that it viewed the outer London boroughs as out of date within a year or two of their creation. The Ministry of Housing and Local Government made no effort to pay lip-service to the principle that town and country should be governed separately; instead it proposed the creation of city-region authorities, uniting a city and its surrounding suburbs and quasi-suburbs with rural areas beyond.[12] Even the organizations representing county and borough councils were prepared to see significant change. The C.C.A. spoke of 500,000 as a desirable minimum population for new top-tier authorities to run most of the major services, while the A.M.C. wanted most

[12] This suggestion followed closely the known opinion of one member of the commission. Before his appointment, Mr. Derek Senior had for some years put forward the view that local government should be reformed on the basis of the city region. He felt sufficiently strongly about this to dissent from the proposals of his colleagues on the commission, and he produced a lengthy memorandum of dissent (Cmnd. 4040, Vol. 2). In this he proposed the creation of thirty-five city-regional authorities with 148 district councils beneath them.

functions to be given to a second tier which would normally cover a combined town and country area and have a population of at least 200,000.

Despite the inconclusiveness of the objective research, the commission took advantage of the general atmosphere which surrounded its work and reached quite different conclusions about the size of a local authority from those found in the Herbert Report. These were of two kinds. First, the commission was convinced that the town–country dichotomy should be ended for those *environmental* services which depended on suitable geographic areas—town planning, highways and transportation, major development, fire, police. It refrained from proposing new areas which were completely urbanized, and proposed the inclusion of large rural tracts in the area of new authorities based on the conurbations, as well as a union of town and country in the less urbanized parts of England. The authority based on Manchester, for example, was to extend for more than 20 miles from the city centre and covered large parts of Cheshire and the Peak district; that around Birmingham would bite deeply into Worcestershire and Staffordshire. Norwich would include most of Norfolk, while the market gardens of the Fylde would join with Blackpool.

The commission's second conclusion was that 250,000 (plus or minus) was the minimum population size of authority for effectively running the education and social services. These were seen as *personal* services dependent more on case-loads and financial resources than on geography, though they too should be administered over mixed urban and rural areas wherever possible. As with the Herbert Commission, there was no exact scientific base for this proposal which was one of subjective judgement rather than statistical measurement. The commission found the evidence conclusive that only an authority of this size would 'have at its disposal the range and calibre of staff, and the technical and financial resources necessary for effective provision of (education, housing, and the personal services)'.[13]

So far functional effectiveness has been discussed only in terms of the size of a local authority. The third criticism of the old structure of local government was aimed at its complexity, and one aspect of this was the division of responsibility between county and district. The Redcliffe-Maud Commission viewed this as not just a problem of complexity. It was convinced that the inherent links between

[13] Cmnd. 4040, para, 257.

local government services were such that divided responsibility meant functional ineffectiveness.

The commission argued as follows. One authority should be responsible for land-use planning and transportation. It could be effective only if it had positive development powers, and it should therefore also be the housing authority. At the same time the Seebohm Committee (on the personal social services) had reached a firm conclusion that one single authority should administer the housing, education, and personal social services. Other services such as libraries, fire, and police were brought into the argument in similar fashion. The only final conclusion that could be drawn was that a single all-purpose authority was 'local government in its simplest, most understandable and potentially most efficient form'.[14]

This added a new dimension to the debate about functional effectiveness, and led the commission to propose the creation of all-purpose *unitary* authorities wherever possible. These new authorities must satisfy its criteria in respect of size: an area embracing town and country and a population of at least some 250,000. Fifty-eight unitary authorities were proposed.

Around Liverpool, Manchester, and Birmingham, however, the commission found conclusive reasons for proposing special arrangements. If there were unitary authorities for each of these areas, they would have to cover populations of between 2,000,000 and $3\frac{1}{4}$ million and areas of 600 to well over 1,000 square miles. Such authorities, the commission felt, would be unsuitable if they were the sole organ of local government for all purposes. Further, each was large enough to be subdivided into boroughs of sufficient size and population to be made responsible for all the main personal services. In these three *metropolitan areas* it therefore proposed a two-tier system, with the top tier responsible for the environmental services of planning, transportation, and major developments, and a second tier of metropolitan districts (twenty in all) large enough to run the personal services of education, housing, and welfare. This distribution of responsibilities was rather similar to the new structure in London, with strategic planning and transportation functions entrusted to the G.L.C., and housing, education, and social services to the boroughs.

[14] Cmnd. 4040, para. 253.

THE SEARCH FOR DEMOCRATIC VIABILITY

One reason why the Redcliffe-Maud Commission did not recommend unitary authorities for the metropolitan areas was that it saw the possibility of 'serious managerial problems due to the sheer size and complexity of the organisation'.[15] But it confessed that it had very little evidence to suggest that large authorities like the (former) L.C.C. or the Lancashire County Council suffered from diseconomies of scale. Its conclusion that 'around one million' was about the right maximum size for a unitary authority for organizational and managerial reasons therefore claimed no justification on empirical grounds.

A much more important set of reasons for the rejection of massive unitary authorities reflected the commission's concern to achieve 'a viable system of local democracy'. In defining what constituted such a system the commission followed a similar approach to that of the Herbert Commission. First, both bodies were convinced of the need for a minimum size of authority on democratic as well as technical grounds. An elected councillor in a very small authority had too little to do and might well be more closely involved in the running of services than was desirable. Secondly, it was questionable whether elected members could cope with the problems of a very large authority, and the right balance between the roles of officers and councillors might also be unobtainable there.

The Redcliffe-Maud Commission put it this way:

For democratic control to be a reality, the size of authority must be such that the elected representatives can comprehend the problems of the area, determining priorities and taking decisions on policy in full understanding of the issues at stake.[16]

This has implications both for the population size of an authority, since a councillor ought not to represent too large an electorate if he is to be responsive to its needs and attitudes, and also for its geographical area, which ought to be one in which the inhabitants have a common interest, with an administrative centre reasonably accessible both to the public and to the councillor.

Both royal commissions discussed the problem of population size in terms of representation. The Herbert Commission produced tables showing the population to be represented by each councillor

[15] Cmnd. 4040, para. 270.   [16] Cmnd. 4040, para. 273.

under the structure which it was considering. It made no specific recommendations about the size of electorate that a councillor should represent, but was satisfied that its proposed fifty-two boroughs would be democratically viable. The Redcliffe-Maud Commission was more positive and recommended that the new authorities be elected through single-member constituencies. It calculated that the use of this method, rather than the multi-member electoral divisions hitherto used in boroughs, would result in few councillors representing more than 10,000 people,[17] a figure which compared favourably with the existing position in the larger county and county borough councils.

The Redcliffe-Maud Commission also placed more emphasis on the geography of reform than did its predecessor in London. The Herbert Commission, reviewing a totally urbanized area in which the average local authority already had a population close to 90,000, made proposals under which twenty of the fifty-two new boroughs would consist of a single existing authority with a new status. The commission in any case regarded its map as tentative: it was more concerned with the arguments of principle about a new council for Greater London and new most-purpose London boroughs than with recommending definite areas.

By contrast the Redcliffe-Maud Commission spent much time and energy on the detailed geography of reform. It was dealing with more than a thousand existing authorities of all types and sizes, from the large county through cities and smaller towns to remote rural districts. Its views on the desirability of unitary authorities with a population of at least 250,000 meant that wholesale reorganization would be necessary. The commission was determined to propose a detailed pattern of areas in order to demonstrate that its principles were practical and give the Government no excuse for deferring action.[18]

Two types of research relevant to this task were undertaken. A national sample survey of 'community attitudes' found that people thought of their local community as a quite small area—a village or small town and, if they lived in a larger town, as a ward or group of

[17] It proposed a maximum council membership of seventy-five. This meant that only councillors in the three metropolitan areas and in two metropolitan districts and twelve unitary authorities would represent, on average, more than 10,000 people.

[18] The commission's terms of reference specifically instructed it 'to make recommendations . . . for authorities *and boundaries* . . . having regard to the size and character of *areas* . . .' (authors' italics). Cmnd. 4040, Vol. 1, p. iii.

streets. On the other hand research into objective criteria such as patterns of journeying to work, migration, and newspaper circulation suggested the existence of communities (areas with common interests) which spread well beyond a town into the surrounding countryside.

Both the subjective and the objective evidence was used by the commission in formulating its detailed proposals. The former was cited in support of a recommendation that grass-roots authorities (known as local councils) be created. These would act chiefly as representational bodies and have few executive functions. A local council would in the first instance cover the area of an existing parish, urban district, or borough.

The objective evidence was heavily drawn upon by the commission in delimiting unitary and metropolitan areas. The commission was concerned to create areas with common interests and to base the new authorities on a central town in order to make them as accessible to the public and to elected members as possible. Indeed more than a third of its main report consisted of a detailed geographic description of each of the proposed new authorities.

Important though social geography was to the Redcliffe-Maud Commission, it was not often allowed to override the population criteria (of about 250,000 minimum and 1,000,000 maximum). Three unitary authorities contained more than 1,000,000 inhabitants, but only marginally: Sheffield, the largest, had a population of 1,081,000. Three, together with two metropolitan districts, fell below 250,000: the smallest (Halifax) had a population of 195,000. At both upper and lower limits the commission had to balance the argument based on social and geographic facts against that based on population size. For example, it chose to amalgamate Bury and Rochdale instead of creating two separate metropolitan districts because the latter decision would mean that neither area 'would have the population or resources to be an effective main authority'.[19] On the other hand, it divided Kent because the existing county, with a population of 1·3 million, was well above the maximum limit, though it had to admit that 'our socio-geographic evidence does not suggest that Kent lacks coherence'.[20] Finally, wherever possible, existing traditional boundaries were preferred to completely new ones.

Thus three major inquiries into the structure of local government took place between 1957 and 1969. The Local Government Com-

[19] Cmnd. 4040, p. 225.   [20] Ibid., p. 295.

mission was given terms of reference and a statutorily defined procedure which effectively restricted its work to a consideration of only marginal changes. Except in the major conurbations it could not propose the creation of a new type of local authority, and even there the geographical limits of the conurbations were narrowly defined. The changes which resulted from its work were therefore restricted largely to a number of county borough boundary extensions and an amalgamation of counties in mid-Anglia. The two royal commissions were given wider briefs (though the boundary of Greater London might well have been more broadly defined), and both seized the opportunity to produce reports favouring wholesale change. Both sought to strengthen the structure of local government in order to make the system both functionally and democratically more viable. It is now time to consider the fate of their reports and outline the new structure which emerged from the debate about their recommendations.

4

The New Structure

By a remarkable coincidence the timetable of events following the reports of the Herbert Commission in 1960 and the Redcliffe-Maud Commission in 1969 was virtually identical. Within three years of each report Parliament had passed major laws which established a new structure of local government, first for London and then for the rest of England and Wales. A year later the new authorities were elected. After a year of existence as shadow councils, preparing to run the local services, the new authorities became fully operational. The whole process covered a five-year period in each case.

Another similarity lay in the treatment that the two reports received. Neither was implemented unchanged: indeed major recommendations in both reports were severely amended by the government of the day (Conservative in the first case and Labour, and then Conservative, in the second), either in its first review of the proposals leading to the publication of a White Paper, or in the period between the White Paper and the presentation of a bill, or even during the passage of the bill through Parliament. In both cases the Government accepted certain major principles on which the two commissions based their reports but departed substantially from them in practice. Its choice was limited, for besides considering on their merits the reactions of local authorities and other interested parties to the two reports it was bound to take account both of the possibilities of putting through Parliament a major reform of local government and of the political consequences that might follow.

Naturally enough, most local authorities reacted unfavourably to proposals for their abolition or amalgamation. In London the most

bitter opponent of the Herbert Commission's proposals was the
London County Council. It could reasonably claim to be one of the
most progressive and effective local authorities in England, or
indeed in the world. Yet here was a proposal for its planning,
transportation, fire, and ambulance services to be taken over by a
new council for Greater London, and for its education, health,
welfare, and children's services to be fragmented. Middlesex
County Council similarly faced abolition, while the other county
councils (Essex, Kent, Surrey, and Hertfordshire) were asked to
lose large areas to the new Greater London Council. The three
county boroughs (Croydon, East and West Ham) were reluctant
to forfeit their independent status. However, there were some
authorities in the area who favoured the report, particularly the
larger district councils which were to take over responsibility for
major services either without any boundary changes or after amalgamation with a smaller neighbour.

It was even harder to find support for the Redcliffe-Maud plan
among local authorities. Urban and rural districts were to be
abolished; many counties were to be carved up; all county boroughs
would lose their independent status and most of them would have
only a minority of voters in the proposed unitary authorities. Even
so, some counties and county boroughs favoured the plan; but most
did not, with the result that not one of the powerful national
associations of local authorities came out in support of the report.
The proposed new authorities were attacked as being either too
large and remote for democratic purposes or too small for effective
planning.

The political balance sheet which each government of the day
had to consider was more complicated. First, there was the attitude
of Members of Parliament, particularly of those within the governing party—the Conservatives in 1960, when the report on London
was published, and during the next four years; the Labour Party in
1969, the year of publication of the report on England, and for the
next twelve months; and the Conservatives from 1970 until the
establishment of the new structure. An important consideration
was the effect of reform on parliamentary constituency boundaries (which would in due course be brought into line with any
new local authority boundaries). In 1970 this particularly worried
a number of Conservative members with rural seats, as the proposed
boundaries in the Redcliffe-Maud Report tended to divide rural
areas. Another major concern of M.P.s was with constituency

opinion, and many members were put under great pressure by their local parties to fight the plans.

Secondly, the Government had to consider the timing of any legislation. Here again there were two implications. First, to legislate shortly before a general election could give a new government the chance to revoke the new law before it came into force. This was a particular problem for the Conservatives in 1960, and there are signs that they pressed ahead at full speed in order to get the new authorities in London elected before the general election due in 1964 for fear that the Labour Opposition might cancel the reform if it were returned to power in time. The Redcliffe-Maud Report, on the other hand, could not possibly become law before the next general election (due in 1971 at the latest). The second implication of the legislative timetable concerned public reaction to local government reform. This issue is not unreasonably regarded as one which can only lose votes for the party proposing reforms, and here therefore is a further argument against legislating too near a general election. In 1963 the Conservative Government decided that on balance it should legislate and risk the consequences, in order to achieve a new London structure which it favoured. No such choice was available to the Labour Government in 1969. It was anxious to implement most of the Redcliffe-Maud Report, but clearly it could legislate only if returned to power at the coming general election.

Another major factor in the balance sheet was the likely political control of the new authorities. In London the fact that the new G.L.C. was as likely to be controlled by the Labour Party as by the Conservatives did not deter the Government from proceeding with reform. This may have been because the L.C.C. which the G.L.C. was to replace had been permanently under Labour control. The outcome of elections to the Redcliffe-Maud authorities was even more difficult to predict, for in many parts of the proposed areas there had hitherto been no party political candidates in local elections. Neither of the major parties could feel confident that it would benefit politically from the adoption of the commission's report, but perhaps the Conservatives were less inclined than Labour to expect advantage from drastic change, because the report was published at a time when three years of bad election results for the Labour Party had put virtually all the existing councils under Conservative control.

THE NEW STRUCTURE IN LONDON

Modifications made to the Herbert Report by the Conservative Government reflected these various pressures. Three major sets of changes to the proposed structure were made between the publication of the report in 1960 and the passing of the London Government Act in 1963.

First, the outer boundary of Greater London was drawn tighter. Nine district councils which had been proposed for inclusion in Greater London by the commission managed to get themselves moved out. Most of these were the solidly Conservative outer suburbs, which were hostile to the idea of being absorbed in 'London' and put great pressure on the Government through their local authorities, M.P.s, and party officials.

The second set of changes was in the size of the new London boroughs. The commission had proposed fifty-two, with populations from around 100,000 to 250,000; but the Government took the view that these were too small to provide the education service and, further, rejected the commission's compromise suggestion for splitting responsibility for education between the G.L.C. and the boroughs. It therefore opted for boroughs with populations of between 150,000 and 350,000 with a minimum of 200,000 wherever possible. Thirty-two London boroughs were established as a result.

The third major alteration also concerned education, but only in the inner area of London (the old L.C.C. area). The L.C.C., supported by the London Teachers' Association, the Labour Party, and many others, protested strongly that to fragment its service would lead to a fall in standards. Undoubtedly there was support for this view both within the Ministry of Education and within the Government. The 1961 White Paper therefore acknowledged that the administrative problems of dividing the service between several boroughs in the centre of London were almost insurmountable, and suggested that an education authority covering about 2,000,000 people in the central area 'might be appropriate'.[1] Following further pressure this area was extended and became identical with that of the L.C.C., covering more than 3,000,000 people. Thus the L.C.C. education service was reprieved. It is now run by a body known as the Inner London Education

---

[1] Ministry of Housing and Local Government, *London Government: Government Proposals for Reorganisation*, Cmnd. 1562 (H.M.S.O., 1961), para. 41.

Authority (I.L.E.A.), which is a special committee of the G.L.C., consisting of all G.L.C. councillors who represent the area together with one member from each of the twelve Inner London boroughs and one from the City of London.

These by no means exhaust the points at which the commission's proposals were modified. For example, the boroughs were given increased planning powers and the G.L.C. rather more parks and open spaces than the commission had envisaged. But it was arguments about the size of boroughs and the education service that caused most debate.

The final allocation of functions between the G.L.C. and the thirty-two London boroughs in the 1963 act illustrates the importance of the boroughs (see Table 3).

TABLE 3. *Distribution of functions in London under the 1963 act**

G.L.C.	London Boroughs
Fire	Personal health services
Ambulance	Welfare services
Refuse disposal	Children's service
Land drainage	Libraries
Smallholdings	Refuse collection
Thames Flood Prevention	Swimming-baths
Motor-vehicle and Driving Licences	Weights and Measures
	Food and Drugs
	Public health inspection and sanitation
	Cemeteries and Crematoria
	Collection of Rates

Shared Services

G.L.C.		London Boroughs
I.L.E.A. in Inner London	*Education*	20 Outer London boroughs
Main roads	*Roads*	Minor roads
Strategic plan	*Planning*	Local plans and most development control
Overspill plus the L.C.C.'s 220,000 houses	*Housing*	Full housing powers
L.C.C. parks	*Parks*	Full powers
Main sewers and sewage disposal	*Sewage*	Sewers, apart from main ones
Over-all traffic authority; approves schemes	*Traffic*	Car parks; road signs and marking

* Several minor functions are excluded.

Subsequent developments have amended this table in several respects. The Local Authority Social Services Act of 1970 led to the fusion of welfare, children's, and parts of personal health services

into new borough social services departments. Other parts of the
personal health services, and ambulances, were transferred to the
new regional and area health authorities in 1974. In the same year
flood prevention, sewage disposal, and land drainage became the
responsibility of the new regional water authority.

Another change, in 1970, had handed over to the G.L.C. responsibility for the buses and tubes in the metropolis. For many
years these had been under public control but had hitherto been the
responsibility not of an elected local authority but of London Transport, a board specially appointed by central government and operating through an executive of paid officers. Under the new arrangements day-to-day running of the transport services has remained
with this executive but the G.L.C. is responsible for policy.

Some of the shared services are gradually being reorganized. In
1971 several G.L.C. parks and 46,000 of its houses were transferred
to the boroughs and 5,700 houses followed in 1972. Other developments may further strengthen the G.L.C.'s role in relation to highways and traffic control where, already, an act of 1969 has transferred certain powers (e.g. over traffic signs and zebra crossings)
from the central government to the council: provisions in that act for
the G.L.C. to take over full responsibility for principal roads in Outer
London, however, have still not been implemented by the Minister.

THE METROPOLITAN AREAS OUTSIDE LONDON

The Redcliffe-Maud Report recommended the creation of three new
top-tier authorities covering the West Midlands, Merseyside, and
Greater Manchester conurbations. The commission strongly contested the traditional separation of town and country, and its three
metropolitan areas reflected the view that any new authorities
should cover both a town area and its semi-rural and rural hinter-
land. They were to include not only built-up areas but also surrounding land up to a further distance of 20 or 30 miles. In this
respect they differed from the almost wholly urbanized area of the
G.L.C.

Despite loud opposition from numerous small towns and rural
districts and from several county councils which would disappear or
lose much territory to the new metropolitan areas, the Labour
Government accepted these proposals in February 1970.[2] This

[2] Ministry of Housing and Local Government, *Reform of Local Government in
England*, Cmnd. 4276 (H.M.S.O., 1970).

White Paper added a fourth metropolitan area in West Yorkshire, based on Bradford, Leeds, Halifax, Huddersfield, and Wakefield, and a fifth in South Hampshire, embracing the Southampton–Portsmouth area. Four months later came a general election (in which local government reform was hardly mentioned) and a change of government.

The Conservative opposition's cautious reaction to the February 1970 White Paper had been critical of it on two grounds. First, the new authorities, both metropolitan and unitary, would be too remote from the public. Secondly, the threat to the continued existence of certain county councils which were providing good services must be resisted. Cheshire and Lancashire were singled out in particular by the opposition spokesman, Mr. Peter Walker, in a debate in the House of Commons on the White Paper. Neither county council would exist under the proposals of the Labour government and the commission. Cheshire would be divided between the Greater Manchester and Merseyside metropolitan areas, and a unitary authority based on Stoke; Lancashire between these same metropolitan areas, and five unitary authorities in the northern part of the county.

The Conservative Government's White Paper reflected its pledge to these and other counties.[3] It proposed a new two-level structure of local government based on existing counties wherever possible. The town–country dichotomy would be ended by the abolition, as the commission had proposed, of county borough status. Pressure from county areas (where the Conservative Party is often at its strongest) and from district councils had led to a major change of policy.

But the concept of the metropolitan area was retained by the Conservative Government, and six such counties were proposed. To the commission's original three were added West Yorkshire; South Yorkshire, based on Sheffield and Doncaster; and Tyne and Wear, including Sunderland as well as Newcastle. But the outer boundaries of these metropolitan counties were to be drawn much more tightly than the commission had envisaged and would embrace little more than the built-up conurbation. Nearby counties like Cheshire, Lancashire, Worcestershire, and Staffordshire were to retain many of their towns and villages. In Cheshire these included Winsford, Northwich, Knutsford, Macclesfield, and Lymm. During

---

[3] Department of the Environment, *Local Government in England: Government Proposals for Reorganisation*, Cmnd. 4584 (H.M.S.O., 1971).

the passage of the bill through Parliament in 1971–2 additional changes reduced the size of several metropolitan areas still further: for example, the transfer of Skelmersdale, Whitworth, Wilmslow, and the large parishes of Poynton and Hale strengthened Cheshire and Lancashire at the expense of Merseyside and Greater Manchester.[4]

The metropolitan districts remain more or less as conceived by the Redcliffe-Maud Commission. The minimum population figure of 250,000 was accepted by both Labour and Conservative Governments; but in consequence partly of the constricted boundaries of the metropolitan counties, partly of political pressure to divide proposed districts such as Bury–Rochdale and St. Helens–Huyton, rather more of the districts fall below 250,000 than was suggested in the original proposals.[5]

The metropolitan county councils, elected in 1973 and operative from 1974, are shown in Table 4.

TABLE 4. *Metropolitan counties: size and division into districts*

Name	1973 Population (thousands)	Number of Metropolitan Districts
1. Greater Manchester	2,722	10
2. Merseyside	1,651	5
3. South Yorkshire	1,320	4
4. Tyne and Wear	1,209	5
5. West Midlands	2,790	7
6. West Yorkshire	2,064	5

The physical characteristics of these new counties make them rather similar to Greater London. The similarity is even closer when account is taken of the responsibilities of county and district respectively. The county is responsible for strategic planning and the making of a 'structure plan'; for the construction and maintenance of major roads; for passenger transport (with an executive of officers to handle day-to-day administration as in London); for the fire brigade; and for police (in London not a local government responsibility). It has certain reserve housing powers, probably only to be used for overspill and town-development schemes, and is also

[4] Map 1 on pp. 176–7 compares the Redcliffe-Maud Commission boundaries for the north-west with those of the 1972 act.

[5] See the map of the metropolitan districts in the Greater Manchester county on p. 178.

responsible for refuse disposal (though not collection). A list of its functions is in Table 5 (p. 51).

The districts, as in London, are the major service providers. Education, housing, the social services, libraries, parks, local planning, and most public health functions are their business. This means that they determine the great bulk of local government expenditure, and they collect the rates on behalf of the metropolitan county.

THE REST OF ENGLAND

From 1974 the whole of England has been covered by county councils, with district councils beneath them. Thirty-nine county and 296 district councils now provide all the local government services outside London and the six other conurbations.

This basic philosophy of two-tier government through new county and district councils has produced outside the metropolitan areas a structure of local government which today bears a marked resemblance to that in existence before 1974. But six major changes were in fact made by the 1972 act, as follows:

(1) All-purpose county boroughs were abolished and the larger towns now form part of the new counties.

(2) In three parts of the country entirely new administrative counties have been created: Cleveland, based on Teesside; Avon, based on Bristol and Bath; Humberside, based on Hull but including land south of the Humber in north Lincolnshire. Unlike the great majority of the new counties, these are not based on the historic shires.

(3) In order to achieve units of 250,000 population, several small counties have been amalgamated with their neighbours (for example Rutland, Herefordshire, Westmorland).

(4) To reflect current and prospective trends of social and economic life, boundary changes between counties have been made in several places. For example, part of Lancashire has joined Westmorland and Cumberland (now called Cumbria); Gatwick Airport has moved from Surrey into West Sussex, as has a wide strip of land between Crawley and Brighton, formerly in East Sussex.[6]

(5) There have been wholesale amalgamations of districts, so

[6] See the map of the new counties (including the metropolitan counties) on p. 179.

that in the thirty-nine new counties there are now only 296, where there were formerly around 930. The areas of some larger towns (including twenty-eight of the former county boroughs) remain as before, but most districts consist of two or more former boroughs, urban or rural districts. Small and medium-sized towns are now merged with their surrounding rural areas.[7] Almost all the districts have populations of over 40,000, and the average is around 90,000. Their boundaries were drawn up by the Local Government Boundary Commission, which now has the continuing task of keeping local authority boundaries and electoral areas, county and district, up to date.

(6) Parish councils and parish meetings are the only elements in the old local government structure that continue as before. But in addition small towns were given the choice of having a parish-type council and some 250 decided to continue their existence in this way, as well as becoming part of a new district.

Formidable though this list of changes may be, it was far less drastic than would have followed full implementation of the Redcliffe-Maud Report, whether as originally presented or as modified by the Labour Government.

The functions exercised by the new counties and districts today also bear some relation to those of pre-1974. In marked contrast to metropolitan areas, where the district has much heavier duties than the county, elsewhere it is the county council that is responsible for the bulk of services: education, social services, transportation policy, libraries, refuse disposal, police, and fire. It also draws up the strategic structure plan for use of land throughout the county. District councils have chief responsibility for housing and the local environment, but for the rest their powers are less glamorous: local plan-making and development control, public health, refuse collection, parks, museums, and recreation are examples. Table 5 illustrates the distribution of the major functions in both metropolitan and non-metropolitan areas.

The blurred nature of the division of responsibility for several services is all too obvious. Some, like parks, museums, and swimming baths, can be provided by either county or district councils. Highways, depending on their importance as traffic arteries, may be maintained by either. Town and country planning is particularly difficult to describe precisely, for the details were left to the new councils to work out locally and it will be some time before the

[7] See the map of the districts in Cheshire on p. 180.

TABLE 5. *Distribution of functions under the 1972 act**

ALL COUNTY COUNCILS	ALL DISTRICT COUNCILS
POLICE	HOUSING (i.e. provision and
FIRE	management; slum clearance;
REFUSE DISPOSAL	house and area improvement)
CONSUMER PROTECTION	PUBLIC HEALTH: hygiene;
(e.g. Weights and Measures;	slaughter-
Food and Drugs)	houses;
	smoke control
HOUSING: limited reserve	REFUSE COLLECTION
powers.	ROADS: minor road maintenance;
	car parks
ROADS: construction and	PLANNING: local plans under
improvement;	development plan
traffic control;	scheme;
maintenance of	most development
main roads	control
PLANNING: structure plan;	
development	
plan scheme;	
major development	
control decisions	
NATIONAL PARKS (where	
appropriate)	

OTHER SERVICES

EDUCATION ⎫
SOCIAL SERVICES ⎬ Responsibility of county councils in non-
LIBRARIES ⎭ metropolitan areas; district councils in
metropolitan areas.

TRANSPORT Metropolitan county council is passenger transport
authority; in non-metropolitan areas districts retain
bus fleets subject to county policy.

PARKS ⎫
MUSEUMS AND ⎬ All county and district councils have powers.
GALLERIES
BATHS ⎭

* Several minor functions are excluded.

final pattern is clear. All counties are responsible for the county structure plan; all districts handle the bulk of planning applications, though certain applications of major importance are reserved for county decision. It is in making local plans that most uncertainty remains. Here the county council, in consultation with its districts, has to draw up a 'development plan scheme' which lists what local plans are to be made, when, and by whom. Some disagreements are almost inevitable over the contents of this scheme.

The division of labour between county and district also varies from one area to another according to the use made of a clause in the 1972 act allowing councils to use 'any other local authority' for the discharge of certain functions. In theory there is no necessity for this provision (commonly called 'agency') to be used at all, for it is only permissive and not mandatory. But the chief reason for its inclusion in the act was to allow former county boroughs to continue to run certain services as the agent of the county council: their libraries or consumer protection services, for example, though not police, education, or the social services, which were expressly excluded. County councils were expected to make this concession real, and guidelines were sent out to them in a circular from the Environment Department.[8] Under the act district councils were even allowed, if dissatisfied, to appeal to the minister during 1973. Despite the guidelines, about half the district councils made at least one appeal. In many areas, therefore, the exact allocation of work is rather different from that shown in Table 5, especially in districts which were formally county boroughs.

AN APPRAISAL

Attention has already been drawn to five criticisms of the old local government structure: on grounds of the smallness of some authorities, geography, complexity, apathy, and subordination. How far are these faults likely to be corrected by the changes made by the acts of 1963 and 1972?

(1) *Smallness*

The new authorities are certainly larger and fewer than the old. In round figures 400 replaced more than 1,300. On the other hand there are several examples of quite small authorities resulting from reorganization, judged by the criteria suggested both by commissions and by Labour and Conservative governments. A minimum of 250,000 population for the effective exercise of education and social service responsibilities was recommended by the Redcliffe-Maud Commission and endorsed by governments of both political parties. Except for the Isle of Wight, all thirty-nine county education and social service authorities are larger than this, but in the conurbation areas the picture is rather different. Of the twenty Outer London boroughs only eight are large enough; so, too, are only twenty of the

[8] Department of the Environment, *Local Government Act 1972, sections 101 and 110: Arrangements for the Discharge of Functions*, Circular 131/72 (H.M.S.O., 1972).

thirty-six metropolitan districts.[9] And many that are too small are in parts of the country where financial resources are significantly low. Further, in its White Paper the Labour Government had proposed, on grounds of size, to make the metropolitan counties, not the districts, responsible for education, and eventually this change may well be made.

At district council level in the non-metropolitan counties the Government instructed the Local Government Boundary Commission to aim at a minimum population of 40,000. The commission did so in its draft proposals which included no district below the minimum. But there were several objections to the draft scheme, particularly from sparsely populated parts of the country where geographically large districts were proposed. As a result, in its final report (which was completely implemented by the Government) some fourteen of the 296 districts recommended were below the 40,000 minimum, the smallest (Teesdale, the Barnard Castle area of Durham) having fewer than 25,000 inhabitants.

(2) *Geography*

This criticism was made at two levels: that of principle, based on social and economic facts; and that of the practical difficulty of keeping boundaries up to date.

The new structure of the 1972 act was founded on the Government White Paper of February 1971. This clearly accepted the principle of the Redcliffe-Maud Report that town and country should in future be governed by a single authority: 'The division between counties and county boroughs has prolonged an artificial separation of big towns from their surrounding hinterlands for functions whose planning and administration need to embrace both town and country'.[10] Yet the final outcome of the process of reform ensures a continuation of this artificial separation in several parts of England. First, there are places where a major city is near the boundary of the county of which it now forms a part, although its area of influence spreads deep into a neighbouring county. Brighton, Luton, and Plymouth are three such examples. Much more serious, however, are the restricted areas of the G.L.C. and metropolitan counties. Here pressure from existing counties caused the Conservative Governments in 1963 and 1972 to draw metropolitan boundaries

[9] A breakdown of the new authorities by population is given in Appendix 1, p. 170.
[10] Cmnd. 4584, para. 6.

which left as many areas as possible within their traditional limits.

It would be wrong to describe all seven (including the G.L.C.) metropolitan counties as totally urbanized, for there are large parts of both West and South Yorkshire which have a rural character. Yet even these, and still more clearly the other five, have boundaries which maintain the division between town and country and in some places do not embrace even the whole of the built-up conurbation. The boundary of Greater Manchester county, for example, excludes Wilmslow to the south and Whitworth to the north; that of Merseyside excludes Ellesmere Port, Runcorn, and Widnes. Warrington and its environs remain outside both Merseyside and Greater Manchester, while Harrogate and parts of north Derbyshire escaped inclusion in either of the two Yorkshire metropolitan areas. The boundary of Greater London is similarly so drawn as to exclude such towns as Epsom, Esher, and Watford which certainly come within the immediate influence of the metropolis.

It remains to be seen what effect this will have on the area-based services. Cross-boundary liaison in the provision of the fire, police, and passenger transport services will often be necessary and will probably be achieved quite easily. It is less certain whether good relations between metropolitan counties and their neighbours can be maintained when the more controversial decisions arise over slum clearance and overspill housing. In the north-west there has, for example, been a long history of dispute between the City of Manchester and Cheshire County Council. This has caused decisions to be delayed for years and forced central government to become involved as arbitrator—and eventually to take decisions which the two authorities had long failed to make. Many people hoped that a new structure of local government would enable local authorities themselves to handle this kind of problem: one cannot now be optimistic about this outcome of reform.

Within counties numerous less important geographical anomalies also remain, but here the future looks more promising. Where such remain it is only because the Local Government Boundary Commission (and the Government in determining metropolitan districts) decided wherever possible to amalgamate existing local authorities in order to make reorganization of services easier. Several large towns were therefore converted into new districts without a full review although they were anxious for extensions to bring suburbs within their boundaries. All these and other similar cases will be reviewed in due course by the Boundary Commission (which will review London as well as provincial boundaries) and within a decade the worst anomalies should be removed.

(3) *Complexity*

A comparison of Table 6 with that of the old structure on p. 26 indicates that the system of local government today is much less complex than was its predecessor.

TABLE 6. *The present structure of local government in England*

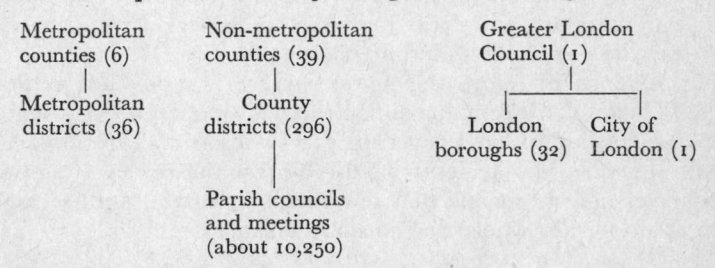

Metropolitan counties (6)	Non-metropolitan counties (39)	Greater London Council (1)
Metropolitan districts (36)	County districts (296)	London boroughs (32) City of London (1)
	Parish councils and meetings (about 10,250)	

But four further factors must be noted which make the new structure rather less simple than the diagram suggests.

First, a number of districts have been allowed to adopt the status of a borough if the whole or a large part of the district formerly consisted of one or more boroughs. This does not affect the allocation of functions in any way, but such areas retain the traditional 'dignified parts' of local government (the mayoralty being the main example). Local government reform has deprived many large cities such as Bristol, Plymouth, and Stoke, of their independent responsibility for education, the social services, and other major functions. In fighting to retain these they succeeded at least in keeping their traditional style.

Secondly, these large towns also managed to obtain responsibility for some parts of major services which the Government originally planned to allocate wholly to the counties. The maintenance of minor roads and local planning powers are the chief examples. At several points therefore it is still impossible for the citizen to know precisely which authority is responsible for what.

Thirdly, the larger towns, especially the former county boroughs, pressed for powers over and above those given to smaller districts. The Government stood firm against this, as the Redcliffe-Maud Commission had done, on the ground that it would fragment county administration and lead to similar demands from growing districts in the future. But it introduced as a concession the so-called agency clause discussed earlier. In consequence the larger county districts commonly act as agents of the county for several services, notably refuse disposal, consumer protection, and highway improvements and maintenance.

The final complexity is inherited from the old system: the use by counties of devolution. But there is a major gain here: the enlarged size of districts has made it easier for county councils to use areas that coincide with only one or two whole districts. They have tended to adopt standard sub-areas for all or most services and to concentrate their area offices in one place.

On balance therefore the new structure is much less complex than the old. Yet it remains difficult to describe largely because the actual operation of local government varies so much from place to place. Further, the widespread use by counties of devolution and of agency powers means that few members of the public can be expected to grasp where decisions are taken.

(4) *Apathy* and (5) *Subordination*

The new structure by itself has less direct effect on these two points of criticism than on the other three. Whether the new authorities evoke a greater response from the public, and whether the degree of central government control is reduced, are questions to which the answers will depend on many other factors than the local government framework. Some of the changes made by the 1972 act, however, may be specially relevant.

First, local elections have been much simplified and now take place on the same day each year. In the past county elections were held in April and other authorities polled on different days throughout a week in May. The new arrangements give the mass media a much better chance of publicizing local elections and this could increase the public's interest in them.

Secondly, the act abolished certain controls over the local councils. Fewer committees, for example, and fewer chief officers are now prescribed by Parliament.

Finally, the Redcliffe-Maud Commission had hoped that the creation of unitary authorities would lead to the early establishment of a single new association able to negotiate with the Government on behalf of all authorities. It hoped that in this way local government would be represented by a stronger body than in the past, when differences of interest between the county councils association, the association of municipal corporations, and the two district council associations weakened the influence of local government on national policy. Any new federal association of authorities may perhaps speak with one voice on many matters, as the old associations often did by issuing joint statements, but on many other local government issues the old conflict of interests seems certain to persist and the three new associations representing counties, metropolitan authorities, and non-metropolitan districts will continue to act independently.

5

Councils and the Community

SOME account has now been given of the services provided by local authorities and of the areas within which they work. It is now time to look more closely at their internal composition and their relations with the local community.

ELECTIONS

All English local authorities with one exception are directly elected. The exception is the very small rural parish with fewer than 200 electors. Though some of these parishes have a directly elected council, most do not, and instead have a parish meeting which all local electors may attend and so take part in parish business. Few parishes of this size have enough work to make the election of a council worthwhile: their business as adviser and critic of higher authority can usually be done satisfactorily by the chairman of the parish meeting or some other local person. Three-quarters of the 10,000 parishes are larger than these tiny hamlets, and they all have a parish council of at least five members.[1]

Four years is the term of office of all councillors, and elections take place on the first Thursday in May, apart from byelections caused by the death or resignation of a councillor.

County councils, the Greater London Council, and the London

---

[1] This is the law but practice may be slightly different. The Redcliffe-Maud Commission found that a small number of parish councils were non-existent because no one had been nominated for election. See Cmnd. 4040, Vol. 3, Appendix 8.

borough councils, like parish councils, have a general election of all members once every four years. For counties and the G.L.C. the relevant years are 1977, 1981, and so on, and the county is divided into electoral divisions, each returning a single councillor. But voting for metropolitan district councils takes place annually (except in years of county elections), with one-third of the members retiring in rotation. These districts are divided into wards which return three councillors, one of whom comes up for re-election each time. Thus electors in metropolitan areas outside London can vote each year: every fourth year for all seats on the county council and in each intervening year for one-third of the seats on the district council.

There is then a uniform pattern of elections to parish, county, and metropolitan district councils. But for non-metropolitan district councils there is less uniformity. The government originally intended that they, like metropolitan districts, should have three-member wards and annual elections of one member. But during the passage of the 1972 act through Parliament the Government was pressed by M.P.s from rural areas and by the rural district councils association to make a change. Traditionally most rural district councils had been elected through single-member divisions (a councillor frequently represented a single village or parish). The new districts were going to be larger than the old and this would mean that a councillor would normally represent more than one village. If he were to be one of a three-member team, this could result in his representing several villages spread over a wide area. The Government responded to these arguments by allowing a district council to choose whether it should be elected *en bloc* every four years or in thirds every year but one, and whether it should have single or three-member wards (or a mixture of these types). A district council which has opted for a general election is elected in 1976, 1979, and then every four years.

These electoral arrangements, particularly those for a standard four-year term of office for all councillors, have not yet come into full effect. The first elections to the new local authorities were in 1973 and in some areas were conducted under temporary arrangements (for example, not all county council electoral divisions were single-member though that is what they will be in future). In that year all councillors were elected but, in order to ease the introduction of the new system, not simultaneously on the first Thursday in May. County councils were elected in April, metropolitan districts in May, and county districts in June. A standard four-year term would have meant that all members retired simultaneously in 1977. This will be true of county councillors but, as noted above, district councillors where the authority has opted for a general election retire in 1976 and then in 1979: only thereafter will the four-year term be the rule everywhere. All metropolitan districts and those county districts that opted for partial rather than general elections poll in 1975, 1976, and 1978, after which the full four-year term will operate (e.g. a councillor elected in 1975 will come up for re-election in 1979).

Two further points about the local government electoral system are worth noting. First, all members of all local authorities are now directly elected, whereas under the old system county and borough councils included among their members a substantial proportion of aldermen who were elected only by councillors.[2] Aldermen were said to provide a council with valuable continuity as they served for six years instead of three. Against this it was argued that their position was undemocratic and that they frequently helped to maintain a party in power which had been defeated at the polls. Their appointment was usually made on political or seniority grounds, and the opportunity to co-opt as aldermen valuable members of the wider local community was seldom taken. These arguments were accepted by the Government, as they had earlier been by the Maud Committee and the Redcliffe-Maud Commission, and the 1972 act abolished the office (except in the City of London where aldermen have long been directly elected).

The second point concerns the revision of electoral areas. In the past, initiative lay with the individual local authority to propose changes. There was therefore a built-in tendency to leave things as they were, since the areas had not proved unsatisfactory to those elected for them; and, although changes were made from time to time, in many areas there were wide disparities between the number of electors in each ward or electoral division.[3] Electoral areas should now be updated more regularly, as the permanent Local Government Boundary Commission is to review electoral arrangements at due intervals.

[2] Aldermen accounted for one-quarter of the membership of county borough, municipal borough, and county councils. In the G.L.C. and London boroughs the proportion is one-seventh until the last London aldermen disappear in 1977.

[3] In one rural district in Rutland each councillor represented one parish. One of them represented nobody as the parish had no population.

This then is the electoral system in English local government. It has not yet had time to settle down but when it does a fairly standard pattern of arrangements will emerge: four-year terms; a fixed date for all local elections; general elections with single-member divisions in counties; partial elections with three-member wards in metropolitan districts; and a mixture of methods in county districts.

VOTERS

Almost anyone over the age of eighteen is entitled to vote at a local election, as also at a parliamentary one. A local official, usually the clerk or chief executive officer of the council, has the duty of drawing up a register of electors each year and making it as accurate as possible. No longer does a resident have to take the initiative in order to be registered. Every house is sent a simple form and householders must return it completed or risk being taken to court. English electoral registers therefore have a high level of accuracy, though inevitably some potential electors are overlooked either by accident (itinerant gipsies for example) or deliberately (some householders may 'forget' tenants for fear of official action against themselves: for example inspection for overcrowding, a higher rateable value if the house is divided into flats, or loss of social security).

As more people have become entitled to vote, so has the proportion actually exercising their right fallen. At one time only ratepayers could register as electors. They had a clear financial interest in the decisions taken by the local authority and election turn-outs were often high. In the last few decades the number of electors has risen sharply as, first, residents who were not direct ratepayers became eligible, and then more recently those aged eighteen to twenty-one. The national average turn-out at local elections shows a steady decline in the period since 1945 from close on 50 per cent to around 35 per cent. Elections to the new authorities in 1973 were slightly better supported (nearly 40 per cent voted at the elections to the forty-five new counties) but this change of trend may be more apparent than real: the first elections to the new London authorities in 1964 and to the new county councils in 1889 were both marked by higher than normal interest, but in neither case did subsequent elections follow a new trend.

Observers have connected the apparent apathy of electors with a variety of causes. The Maud Committee suggested several changes in the electoral system which might increase public interest. Its proposals for the abolition of aldermen and for a single fixed day for all local elections, designed to focus national attention, have now been adopted. The committee also favoured single-member wards and general elections for all authorities, for it felt that too often a local election could not lead to a change of political control as only one-third of the seats on the council were at stake. Its suggestion that candidates should have free postal delivery of their manifestos to all households has not been adopted, though now the compulsory issue of poll cards to all electors by the returning officer at least ensures that everyone knows about a coming election.

Low turn-out, however, probably results from public attitudes to local government rather than from defects in the electoral system. Few people have more than a trivial knowledge of local government or interest in it. Surveys conducted for the Maud Committee and Redcliffe-Maud Commission revealed some startling figures. One in four electors could not spontaneously name a single service provided by their borough or district council. For county councils the figure rose to one in two. Between a quarter and a third thought that county boroughs provided hospitals and electricity, and almost one in five that the clerk of the council was elected.

The cult of personality often characteristic of parliamentary elections is largely missing from local government. Electors in Sheffield were recently asked 'Who do you think is the most important person in local affairs here?' The lord mayor, a civic dignitary with little power, who holds office for only a year, was named by 23 per cent; 17 per cent named a paid official of the local authority; 16 per cent a councillor; and 42 per cent could name no one.[4] Finally, there is no tradition of voting for local councillors, whereas most people make a habit of going to the polls at general parliamentary elections. As a result, around 75 per cent (or twice as many as at local government elections) vote at a general election.

COUNCILLORS

In some areas local elections have been contested by organized political parties for many decades, and there has been a steady increase in the number of councils elected on a party basis in the period from 1918 onwards. The recent reforms of structure have provided a further fillip to local party activity, for in many parts of the country they have brought together towns which have a tradi-

[4] W. Hampton, *Democracy and Community* (O.U.P., 1970), pp. 135-7.

tion of party politics with rural areas which have not. Given past trends it is likely that contests in these rural areas will be increasingly conducted on party lines as the parties active in town areas seek to enlarge their hold on the new councils. This was apparent in 1973. Previously two in five county councillors were 'independents', but in the new counties the proportion dropped to only one in seven.

The important fact about party politics in English local elections is that the chief parties involved are almost always local branches of the major national parties. In many areas there are some purely local parties, ratepayers or tenants associations being the most common, but the bulk of local elections are contested by candidates wearing the familiar Conservative, Labour, or Liberal labels. Local elections thus become contests between the representatives of national parties, and national and local issues become intertwined. Many electors vote for the party rather than the candidate, and there is a certain uniformity in results throughout the country as the national standing of a party prevails over the performance of the local candidate. For example, in 1967–9 the Labour Government was at the height of its unpopularity and Labour candidates in local elections were routed. In 1972 the boot was on the other foot and many Conservative councillors lost their seats because of public reaction to the government of Mr. Heath.

This steady spread of party politics in local elections has had two major effects on the election and composition of councils (as well as further effects on the way councils operate which will be considered later). First, it has increased the number of contested seats. In areas where party politics were slow to develop—many counties and almost all rural districts—the number of seats which returned councillors unopposed was often very large. Throughout the 1960s about half of all county council members and up to three-quarters of rural district councillors were elected without fighting a campaign: the figures in urban areas were around 10 per cent, and much below this in the highly politicized boroughs. The advent of party politics has thus given increasing numbers of people the chance to vote, though their vote has had to be cast for a candidate with a party label.[5] In Devon, for example, the 1970 county council election was contested solely by independent candidates and in fifty-nine of the seventy-five divisions there was no contest. The inclusion of Exeter, Torbay, and Plymouth in the new county altered the position dramatically in 1973. All ninety-eight seats were

[5] In recent years the party of a candidate has been printed on the ballot paper.

contested and only forty-five of the 284 candidates stood under the independent label.

The second effect has been on the composition of local councils and, in general terms, has been that local councils are now somewhat more representative of the communities they serve and govern than they used to be. This change has been specially due to the growth of the Labour Party, for its candidates are more likely to be blue-collar workers than are the Conservatives or independents. Apart from the obvious reason that the party traditionally receives much of its support from such people, there is the fact that the party was the first national one to finance and organize local election campaigns on behalf of candidates.

Despite the change in the social composition of councils resulting from the spread of party politics into local government,[6] most local authorities still fail to reflect proportionately the various elements in the electorate that they represent. A sample survey of nearly 4,000 councillors undertaken for the Maud Committee in 1964 indicated that as many as 54 per cent were over fifty-five years of age (compared to 34 per cent of the voting population), while only 19 per cent were classified as blue-collar (57 per cent of the population fell within this group). The great majority of councillors were farmers, business or professional men, or other non-manual workers, and only 12 per cent were women (who made up more than half the electorate).

Nor can the larger number of contested elections be taken as proof of an increased enthusiasm for service on a local council. Parties have been anxious to fight seats in order to keep their machinery ready for the next general election. Indeed, one reason why the parties have not favoured a general election of local councillors has been that their local organizations would lose the momentum generated by annual campaigns. But all parties have frequently had difficulty in finding sufficient candidates to fight all vacancies, or so the Maud Committee's researchers were told,[7] and public advertisements for candidates have sometimes been issued by parties in the last few years.

The new structure of local government may alleviate this problem.

[6] Documented for a sample of three authorities in the south-east over the period 1930–60 by L. J. Sharpe in British Journal of Sociology,Vol. 13, No. 3, 1962 ('Elected Representatives in Local Government').

[7] Committee on the Management of Local Government, Report (H.M.S.O., 1967), para. 474.

First, now rather fewer councillors are needed than before: some 22,000 instead of 35,000 (excluding parish councillors). For the 1973 elections the parties therefore had to find fewer candidates than there were sitting councillors. In some areas this led to fierce contests within the parties when wards selected candidates, particularly as former aldermen were also looking for seats. Whether such competition continues or not cannot be known, but even in 1973 all the major parties reported a shortage of candidates in some areas.

Secondly, councillors can now claim rather more generous allowances to meet the expenses they incur. Among the alleged deterrents to potential councillors used to be the amount of time which council work involved and the consequence that most councillors were out of pocket. The amount of time may not be much affected by the reform: that will depend on the way councils organize themselves internally, for the bulk of time spent is on council work rather than with constituents, according to figures produced for the Maud Committee. But the financial returns for council service are now greater. Before 1974 'loss of earnings' and travel and subsistence allowances were payable, but only people paid by the hour could easily claim the former. From 1974 a local authority can pay a fixed attendance allowance, subject only to a maximum figure laid down by central government. Though this does not amount to a large annual sum, it may encourage some more people to present themselves as candidates.

The number of potential candidates is in any case rather fewer than the number of voters. Three categories of person on the electoral roll in an area cannot serve as members of the local council. First, those aged between eighteen and twenty-one are not yet eligible. When the voting age was reduced to eighteen, the law relating to candidatures for both parliamentary and local elections was left unchanged. In 1973 the House of Commons Speaker's Conference recommended a change to eighteen for both types of candidate, and if the law is changed accordingly there will be some 2,000,000 extra potential councillors.

A second important disqualification concerns local government officers and other employees. An employee may not and never has been allowed to serve on 'his' local authority, though he can stand for election to the county if employed by a district council and vice versa. In one sense, therefore, every employee is eligible for election but, in another sense, he is half disqualified. Local authorities employ over 2,250,000 people, many of whom have little to do with decisions about the administration of their services and, some argue, it is unfair to prevent any of them from service on their local council. During the passage of the 1972 Local Government Act the Government was put under strong pressure to relax this rule. This it declined to do. If all employees are barred there is no chance that a clash of interests will result from simultaneous service as both employee and councillor, nor will the public have reason to fear that such councillors are serving in order to protect a personal interest of their own. If none is barred, the public image of local government could suffer. The Government argued that any line drawn between the two extremes would be arbitrary and difficult to justify.[8]

A third category of disqualified elector cannot be defined so clearly. This is the elector whom his employer bars from service. Several thousand senior and middle-ranking central government civil servants are the chief example: the political activities of civil servants are restricted in differing degrees depending on their rank. The policy of the public corporations, such as gas and electricity boards, is less definite, though some of their senior officials are either overtly debarred or advised against becoming candidates at local elections. Where the line is drawn varies: in 1972 the B.B.C., for example, told one of its education producers working for Radio Leeds that if elected to the Leeds Metropolitan District Council (an education authority) he would have to resign. The National Union of Journalists fought this decision and the B.B.C. conditionally relaxed its ban.

These three categories together substantially reduce the number of potential councillors below that of electors. But there are two further categories which increase the number of potential members of a council even though they cannot vote at the elections to that council. Anyone who has occupied, either as owner or tenant, land or premises in an area for the past twelve months may stand for election there, even though his name is not on the electoral roll. So too may anyone who for at least a year has regularly travelled into that area to work. This latter group are a recent addition to the number of possible candidates. The change resulted from a recommendation of the Maud Committee and may have made a large addition to the total number of potential candidates, for the 1966 sample census

---

[8] Amendments were unsuccessfully put forward proposing a line drawn between senior officers who actually advise the council and those who merely administer council services. The Government initiated an inquiry into this question in October 1973. See p. 169, fn. 9.

revealed that 34 per cent of the economically active population lived in the area of one local authority and worked in that of another. However, by rationalizing local authority areas the 1972 act has certainly reduced this proportion, and in practice comparatively few commuters are anyhow likely to have close enough links with a local ward to secure adoption as candidates by the ward or divisional party.

COUNCILLORS AND THE COMMUNITY

Local elections are the best-known and most publicized occasions when a local authority comes into direct contact with the people it serves. The ballot-box is the one place where judgement is formally delivered on the past performance of councillors and on promises for the future. But besides this regular machinery there are several other points at which the council and the community are in contact with each other. Collectively these constitute a relationship far more intense and continuous than that of election day.

First, there are relationships initiated by the council, either because of its general legal obligations or because of a particular initiative on its part. At the ceremonial level there is action taken by the mayor or chairman as leading citizen of the community, usually acting in a strictly non-political capacity during his or her term of office. Both mayors and chairmen have in the past done work of real significance in supporting local organizations, attending functions, and initiating charitable campaigns. The first mayor of a new London borough, for example, attended nearly a thousand functions in his year of office and at many of them took the opportunity to remind his audience of the character of the new borough and the need to develop a new loyalty.[9] By allowing many new districts and old boroughs to claim borough status, the 1972 act has ensured that the mayoralty remains a valuable feature of English life.

A local authority can support the activities of voluntary organizations in all manner of ways, and this support is a second point at which councils make contact with their community. Most councils make grants to a wide variety of such bodies, from welfare groups to drama societies.[10] And members of organizations whose work is

[9] Enid Wistrich, *Local Government Reorganisation: the first years of Camden* (Borough of Camden, 1972), pp. 245–6.

[10] In 1971–2 the London borough of Camden, for example, made annual grants totalling £261,000. Some 60 per cent went to bodies providing social and welfare

closely related to council activities may be co-opted to membership of council committees. Such co-option is sometimes statutory— allotment tenants, for example, are entitled to representation on the appropriate committee—but more often it is at the discretion of the council.

There are arguments for and against co-option. It enables a council to make use of experts who have a type of professional knowledge, say of music, which both councillors and officers may lack. Again, the allotment holder has the experience of a consumer; the teachers' representative on an education committee can contribute from experience that neither councillor nor officer may have. Further, co-option provides a valuable link between the council and voluntary organizations or other bodies working in related fields. An old peoples' welfare council, for example, supplements services provided by the council and co-option of a representative to the social services committee can be useful to both partners.

Against this there are disadvantages which cannot be ignored. A co-opted person may fail to consider the wider implications of a policy, however relevant they may be. If co-opted members persuade a committee to recommend some course of action, they cannot speak at the full council meeting—and the recommendation may go by default. Finally, co-opted members have often been selected on party grounds, with no regard for merit but in order to secure their vote. Co-option has in the past been specially prevalent for education and social services committees, and the new authorities have so far tended to follow the broad pattern of the old in this respect.

Thirdly, there have been moves in recent years to make the working of local government more open to public, press, and radio. Before the 1972 act the right of public access was restricted to meetings of the full council, the education committee, and any other committee on which all members of the council served. Further, a motion could be passed to exclude the public and press from the discussion of any part of the agenda that was confidential. However, a council could at its discretion allow people to attend any committees or subcommittees, and some did so.

In one respect the new legislation mirrors the old: a motion can still be passed excluding outsiders from debates on confidential matters. But now the press and public have a right of access to all meetings of committees (though not of subcommittees). A council

services and 35 per cent to arts and cultural organizations. Wistrich, op cit., p. 253.

which wishes to exploit loopholes can of course minimize the effect of this change (e.g. by having fewer committees and more sub-committees), but it invites criticism from the press if it does so. On balance the change means a small net increase in public awareness of council decisions and of how they are reached.

Fourthly, local government has made serious efforts to improve its public relations. The 1972 Bains Report (on management structures for the new local authorities) made much of this and stressed especially the need to inform the public about the new local government system. In the London reorganization of the 1960s little had been attempted, and a survey two years after the birth of the Greater London Council showed that one citizen in three had no idea what the initials G.L.C. stood for. In 1973–4 many councils made real efforts to explain the changes to their citizens: Cheshire, for example, circulated all households twice with details of the new structure and placed half-page advertisements in every local paper circulating in the county. Central government inserted advertisements in the national press and the local government information office made leaflets available to all authorities: well over 1,000,000 copies were distributed.

Finally, a recent innovation in local government has been the Commissioner for Local Administration, known commonly as the Ombudsman. In 1966 Parliament established the post of ombudsman to look into complaints against Whitehall departments. At that time the activities of nationalized industries and other public bodies, including local authorities, were excluded from his terms of reference. But in 1974 two new types of ombudsman were created: one to handle complaints about the National Health Service and one for local government.

The local ombudsman operates on a regional basis and therefore deals with several dozen authorities. Unlike the parliamentary ombudsman, who can investigate only complaints that are referred to him by M.P.s, he can receive a complaint direct from a member of the public, though the latter is expected to show that he has first approached a local councillor. Only complaints of maladministration are investigated, for policy decisions of the council remain the exclusive business of the councillors. Professional freedom for teachers is also guaranteed, for the local ombudsman cannot investigate such subjects as a school curriculum or a school's teaching methods. Nor can he consider disputes where either a minister or a court of law has power to adjudicate. The reports of local ombudsmen are normally published, though none is yet available and for some time it will not be possible to assess the value of this innovation. It may be that, as in the experience of the paliamentary ombudsman, relatively few cases of maladministration are found in local government.

The creation of local ombudsmen was strongly opposed by local government. The associations of authorities asserted that a major task of the local councillor was to handle local grievances and that it had never been shown that he had failed to do this adequately. Against this it was argued that he was too closely involved in the taking of decisions to handle impartially complaints about their consequences. Further, some citizens might not be prepared to bring him a grievance with a highly personal content, particularly if they identified him with the council responsible for it.

It seems clear that local government has little to lose from the creation of ombudsmen. It is to be hoped that they will not be over-employed and will find few grievances of substance. If many cases lead to reports unfavourable to local councils then the ombudsman will be carrying out an important role in helping to make local government more accountable and responsive. Whatever the outcome, there is surely some advantage in having a mechanism for considering complaints which is completely independent of the person complained against.

PARTICIPATION

So much for the initiatives taken by government, local and central, in forging links between the local council and the community. But what initiatives have been taken by the local community itself to improve communications with the local council and influence its thinking and decisions? Throughout the 1960s there certainly was a growing body of dissatisfaction with traditional methods of public participation in local government and much effort has been made to improve them.

Two separate approaches to this question can be made. The first starts from the complaint that too many major policy changes are initiated by a local authority and passed by a committee before the public is aware of them. There will have been consultations and discussions between departments of the local authority before the subject is put to a committee, but seldom will an attempt have been made to consult directly the people chiefly affected—parents and schoolchildren, for example, by a proposed reorganization of schools, or residents in an area proposed for redevelopment. A slightly different type of complaint is that many councils have inadequate devices for obtaining a satisfactory feedback of local views on the running of services. The elected member and the officer both have extensive local contacts, but the former has a multiplicity of roles to fulfil in his spare time while the latter is in a difficult position when asked to express views on questions which have not yet been decided, and he may in any case be concerned only with that aspect of a particular service in which he specializes.

In recent years the growing demand for more adequate consultation with the community has been officially acknowledged by the Government, particularly in relation to planning and housing. In 1968–9 a junior minister, Mr. Arthur Skeffington M.P., chaired an official committee of inquiry into public participation in planning. This committee concluded that 'the essential requirements are that planning authorities should act openly and that the public should react constructively to the facts and ideas put before them', and it recommended the greater use by planning authorities of films, exhibitions, public meetings, and the like.[11]

The Skeffington Committee was particularly concerned with participation during the making of the strategic structure plan but its recommendations were applicable to other situations too. A good example has been the recent policy of renovating whole areas by designating them as general improvement areas (G.I.A.s). For a G.I.A. scheme to succeed, close co-operation from local residents is essential, and authorities have been urged by the Government to 'be tireless in explaining their proposals, and in gaining the confidence and approval of those whom they affect'.[12] In 1969, after legislation had been passed allowing authorities to designate G.I.A.s, a circular from the Ministry recommended that 'the formation of residents' associations should also be encouraged'.[13]

This official concern with participation has been a response to changing circumstances. As local authority services have widened in scope and touched on people's lives more closely, public reaction to officialdom has become more critical. People have objected to

[11] Ministry of Housing and Local Government, *People and Planning* (H.M.S.O., 1969).

[12] Ministry of Housing and Local Government, *Old Houses into New Homes*, Cmnd 3602 (H.M.S.O., 1968), para. 54.

[13] Ministry of Housing and Local Government, *Housing Act 1969: Area Improvement*, Circular 65/69 (H.M.S.O., 1969), para. 23.

the fact that frequently their first opportunity to comment on new local schemes was when an official notice called for objections and promised a formal public inquiry, and that even when an objector was successful he incurred substantial expenses unless he was eventually awarded costs. It was claimed that there were far too few channels of communication between the authority and the citizen. In recent years there has been a notable growth of local pressure groups voicing this criticism, as citizens have sought to show their council the existence of a responsible organization of local opinion that will not be ignored.

There have always been interest groups active in local government, but until recently these have largely been restricted to those of which all members have a similar continuing stake in council activities: teachers' associations and other trade unions, allotment holders and market tenants, or bodies which actually provide services on a voluntary basis, such as the Women's Royal Voluntary Service (W.R.V.S.). All these lack the strict territorial base characterizing the more recent tenants' or residents' associations or civic societies. The first problem for these newer groups has been to gain acceptance by the council as negotiating bodies. But they also often have difficulty in agreeing a common policy, for their members are less evenly affected by new policies than are those of the more traditional groups. Finally, such bodies may lack permanence, especially if they spring up in reaction to a particular event, as did a number of tenants' associations during the controversy over the housing finance act of 1972.

Despite some progress no one can as yet be satisfied with the techniques of participation which have so far emerged. Timing is one of the major problems: if a local authority publicly reveals tentative plans too early, some people may take unfair advantage of them, especially when plans affect future land-use and housing patterns. On the other hand, delay in revealing propsals until they have been well formulated leads to the public reaction that 'this is not consultation', and the exercise appears to be one of public relations rather than participation. A further problem facing the local government officer is that he is often loath to express unofficial support for a new approach to a problem unless he has first tested the views of his elected members, who are naturally jealous of their right to take all policy decisions. Finally, from the point of view of the local group, lack of expertise remains a problem when citizens are talking to professionally qualified officers with a far greater technical knowledge than their own. Unless these officers are positively committed to the idea of consultation and participation, discussions prove unrewarding.

Signs of public discontent with official attitudes have become increasingly apparent and disturbing. The last few years have seen a considerable increase in direct action. An early sign was in the activities of 'squatters', protesting when council houses awaiting redevelopment were left empty. The technique has since spread. There have been mothers jamming dangerous road crossings, council employees on strike, council house tenants withholding rent, and even an isolated case, in London, of schoolchildren holding demonstrations. Within local government there have been signs of some younger officials finding it difficult to balance their official role with their sympathy for public attitudes, particularly in planning and social service departments. Social workers in at least two London boroughs have openly taken sides with their clients against their employer, and the task of the new 'community development officer', employed by the local authority with the specific task of mediation between citizen and council, is fraught with similar hazards.

The new local authorities are in some senses more distant from the communities they serve than were their predecessors. Thirteen hundred authorities have been reduced to 400; the average population and area served has therefore greatly increased. There are rather fewer councillors than before, and the number of direct links between council and community has been reduced. It is for these reasons that some have criticized the new structure of local government as being less democratic than the old.

Before reaching conclusions in this dispute about the democratic viability of the new authorities account must be taken of other developments mentioned in this chapter. In an attempt to make local government more accountable and responsive to its public, the Government has passed new laws opening up committees to the public and establishing a local ombudsman to handle complaints of maladministration. There has been official support from several quarters for better public relations by local authorities, and from the Skeffington Committee and the Government for more public participation in local decision-making.

Despite these parallel developments, it remains impossible to argue that local councils are automatically responsive to local demands and needs. Much depends on the attitude of the particular council and on the efforts made by local communities to argue their point of view. Some councils welcome public involvement in decision-making, others profess to do so but only so long as they remain firmly in control. Some communities throw up strong leadership, others do not. Indeed if this were not the case, there would be less reason to have local government or spend energies in trying to make it work.

6
Councils at Work

THE work for which local councils are elected is to govern: that is, to provide in accordance with the wishes of each local community the services which Parliament has decided that local authorities may or must provide. No council larger than a parish one can do the whole of its work as a single body. Though there are certain acts performed by the county or district council as a whole (and these will be considered later), far the greater part of its work is done by committees: that is, by small groups of members acting on the council's behalf and dealing with particular parts of its total work.

Two principles are usually followed in this division of labour. Some committees administer a single service, education or the social services, for example, on the principle of a vertical division of labour. Others are entrusted with an aspect of the council's work that affects several different services. The finance and establishments (i.e. staffing) committees are examples of this principle, that of a horizontal division.

Traditionally there have been many more vertical committees than horizontal ones in most local authorities, for two reasons. First, the range of services has varied widely over time: some services have been removed from local authority control, some have been added. When a new service has been added, a convenient way to administer it has been by simply creating a new committee. A recent example was the power given to local authorities to declare general improvement areas under the 1969 Housing Act. Some councils (Bury in Lancashire was one) decided to establish an extra committee for this purpose.

The second reason is that Parliament has sometimes obliged local authorities to adopt this approach. The Education Act of 1944, for example, made county and county borough councils appoint education committees. Other acts enforced the appointment of committees for small-holdings, diseases of animals, fire, police, health, and the social services. But there has been only one example of a statutory obligation to appoint a horizontal committee: the old county councils (but authorities of no other type) had to appoint a finance committee.

The 1972 Local Government Act relaxed these statutory obligations and today local authorities have a far greater freedom over their choice of a committee structure than previously. Since 1974 the relevant authorities are still bound to appoint police, education, and social services committees,[1] but the rest of the old legislation has been repealed. In practice the main vertical committees continue, but there has been a strong tendency to group two or more associated services under one committee and so reduce their number. Another trend has been to strengthen the powers of the horizontal committees. Many authoritities now have a senior committee, often called a policy and resources committee, whose job it is to recommend comprehensive objectives and priorities to the council and to co-ordinate executive action.

These recent developments resulted from growing dissatisfaction with the traditional way in which local authorities went about their work. This came to a head in the early 1960s when the local authority associations encouraged the government to establish a committee under the chairmanship of Sir John Maud 'to consider in the light of modern conditions how local government might best continue to attract and retain people (both elected rerpresentatives and principal officers) of the calibre necessary to ensure its maximum effectiveness'. The Maud Committee reported in 1967.[2]

THE MAUD REPORT

The terms of reference of the Maud Committee made no specific mention of local authority committee structures. However, the committee spent much of its time on this aspect of council work because the evidence strongly suggested that local councils were not doing their work as effectively as they might and that this was a

---

[1] National park committees also have to be appointed in the relevant areas.
[2] Ministry of Housing and Local Government, *Report of the Committee on the Management of Local Government* (H.M.S.O., 1967).

deterrent to some potential councillors and officers. More than a quarter of the report was devoted to the internal organization of local authorities, on the ground that 'a more valuable contribution will be made by members and officers if the work of local authorities is organized effectively and managed efficiently'.[3]

The traditional committee system was criticized on several counts. First, it resulted in local authorities having no managing body. There was no underlying concept that one or a few councillors should be responsible for leadership in the direction and control of all the council's activities, and no clear distinction between issues of major and minor importance. Even existing horizontal committees failed to meet these needs: they too dealt with only a specialized part of council work (finance or staffing, for example). The English experience was contrasted sharply with that elsewhere: the mayor or city manager in the United States, the German mayor, the Ontario Board of Control.

A related criticism was that vertical committees were so strong that it was difficult to obtain a council view of needs and services. This was specially important because of the tendency for the committee structure to match the council's departmental structure. For example, the education department and chief education officer would be closely related to the education committee and its chairman, and both would tend to operate independently of the council. Stronger horizontal committees were needed to temper this departmentalism.

Finally, the committee system was time-consuming and costly to run. The average county borough in 1964 had twenty-one committees and forty subcommittees, and members were involved in two meetings a week as a result; officers too had to attend these meetings. Documents flew in all directions: 200 sheets a month or more might reach a county borough councillor. In the counties and districts the number of main committees tended to be rather fewer, reflecting the smaller number of services provided. All the same, a county council was likely to have an even more complicated committee structure than a county borough. Cheshire County Council, for instance, had eighteen committees and fifty-three subcommittees in 1965, and these met on 398 occasions. In addition the system of area committees for certain services meant another sixty-five committees and 479 meetings. The average county councillor served on between nine and ten committees, subcommittees, and area committees.

[3] Op. cit., para. 88.

This diagnosis pointed to two complementary reforms. First, the number of committees should be reduced. Secondly, stronger horizontal committees, possibly coupled with a small managing body of senior councillors, seemed essential if a council was to have effective leadership from its elected members. The Maud Committee followed both of these clues in formulating its recommendations for future committee structures. It proposed the establishment of a Management Board of from five to nine elected members 'to lead and co-ordinate the work of the authority'. Committees would have no executive powers but would be deliberative bodies and report to the management board on the way to the full council. Chief departmental officers too would be responsible, through the clerk, to the board, and the concept of a team of officers under the leadership of the clerk (or chief executive) was stressed. This last aspect of the proposals will be further considered in chapter 7.

This was a radical set of proposals. Indeed, for one member of the committee, Sir Andrew Wheatley, who had long experience as a county clerk, it was too much. He believed that the result of the proposals would be to vest power in the hands of the management board and leave the great majority of elected members with little or no part to play in the formulation of policy. His preference was for committees to continue with executive powers but be reduced in number, and for a management board to deal only with major new policy proposals referred to it by committees.

Though no local authority implemented in full the recommendations of the Maud Committee, many acknowledged the strength of the case for fewer committees and several accepted the need for a strong central one; but this was commonly called a Policy or Co-ordinating Committee, not a management board. By 1970 well over half of all county, county borough, and London borough councils had established a policy committee and two-thirds of these committees had been formed in the period 1968–70.[4]

RESPONSE TO MAUD

It would be wrong to assume that, until the Maud Committee reported in 1967, all councils behaved in quite the way depicted by the committee in its general diagnosis. Criticism of the time-consuming nature of committee work applied to most authorities,

[4] R. Greenwood et al., 'The Policy Committee in English Local Government', *Public Administration*, Summer 1972.

but in differing degree. Many left a host of minor decisions in the hands of officers or committee chairmen and made a conscious effort to reduce committee work to a reasonable minimum. For example, Maud Committee researchers reported that one county council sent out only sixty pages of typescript a month to its members. Another county, and a county borough, had only twelve committees compared with the average of about twenty, and one county borough had a mere three subcommittees. Virtually every authority, however, had a committee structure in the mid-1960s which stood in need of simplification.

There was also undoubtedly much justification for criticisms about the absence of leadership and the difficulties of obtaining a coherent local authority view of policy proposals and service provision. Even so, many authorities had developed techniques designed to offset these weaknesses well before the Maud Committee was appointed.

First, some authorities had for years had some kind of a policy committee. In the survey cited above, ten of the 123 local authorities which replied to the questionnaire had had such a committee since before 1965. In the early 1950s Liverpool's General Purposes Committee had the following task: 'to consider and decide all matters or questions of principle and policy connected with the various activities of the corporation in which more than one of the standing committees of the council are, or are likely to be, concerned'. Manchester's Co-ordinating Committee had a similar function at the time, while Coventry's Policy Advisory Committee had 'the general duty of advising the council in matters of improved administration and improved co-ordination; and in particular on the best course to adopt in the general interests of the city in regard to schemes involving new expenditure (i.e. expenditure not covered by the current estimates) which other committees desire to bring before the council'.

Secondly, some councils had clerks who played an important co-ordinating role, a topic to be explored in Chapter 7. Administrative leadership could on occasion reduce the problem of obtaining a general view of policies at elected member level, though at the risk that officers might in consequence undertake functions more appropriate to the elected member.

Finally, party politics dominated the working of the council in many authorities, including most of the larger ones. Here the parties modelled themselves (as they still do) upon the parliamentary system: the majority party assumed full responsibility for the administration and for all policy decisions. In such authorities both the majority and the minority parties are organized as groups and hold private meetings to discuss council affairs. Often, especially in counties where meeting places are sometimes difficult to arrange, the groups actually meet in the town or county hall, and in some authorities they are recognized as such an integral part of the organization that their meetings are mentioned in the council's official year book or calendar. The party group has its own officers —chairman, secretary, whip—and may have an executive committee. In some councils the chairman of the majority group is formally designated leader of the council. He leads the group in council debate and is generally recognized as having special responsibility in the conduct of council business.

The effect of party organization on the work of the local authority can be seen at several points. First, the majority party normally exercises control by nominating all the committee chairmen and ensuring that it has a majority of the members of each committee. But it is impossible to make statements about styles of government which are true of all authorities. The degree of party control varies widely, from the almost total domination found in London and the big cities to many smaller authorities where party politics are mainly apparent only at election time. In these latter, though the majority party on the council is unlikely to leave any of the more important committees under the control of its opponents, it does not necessarily claim all the chairmanships.

Secondly, party groups meet in private a few days before each council meeting and consider the recommendations of the various committees. The minority party will decide which of these recommendations it wishes to challenge in council (that is, in public with reporters present), and how it will handle the debate: the general line of attack, the order of speaking, and so on. Naturally the group will choose for public discussion matters on which it believes it can make political gain at the expense of its opponents, and in consequence committee recommendations which seem to the ordinary ratepayer the most important are not necessarily discussed at all if they have only limited party-political content. The majority party, in its pre-council meeting, has to decide whether it wishes to alter any committee recommendation. If so, its committee chairman must move in full council that part of his committee's report be deleted or referred back for further consideration. This will suggest to the opposition, and to knowledgeable observers such as the press, that he has run into difficulties with colleagues in his group. The group decision will therefore generally be to go along with the committee recommendations. The group meeting also gives an opportunity for members to ask questions about the recommendations of committees on which they do not serve, so that divisions in the party front may not appear in public.

Thirdly, the party group may also meet on other occasions. In some authorities, the group members will meet privately before a committee meeting to discuss the agenda, a practice which has become more common now that committees, as well as council meetings, are open to press and public. In most authorities, groups discuss major issues in private before these go to committee for decision. A wise committee chairman foresees when an issue requiring decision is likely to be controversial and takes it to the group before allowing the officers to put it on a committee agenda, so that the party line may be clear from the outset.

Thus there exist parallel arrangements for decision-taking. One is formal: it proceeds through the officer of a department to a committee and from there to the council chamber. The other is the more important one, proceeding from the party's committee-men to the full party group and thence to the council chamber. Council meetings held in public tend therefore to be ritualistic: only on those occasional issues where the parties allow a free vote (fluoridation of water supplies has sometimes been an example) does the outcome depend on open and realistic debate.

This whole method of decision-taking can be criticized on the ground that most council activities are basically not party political, that the group system leads to excessive secrecy and, more important still, that a party group takes decisions on insufficient evidence because the council's officers cannot be present to give professional advice. In an effort to meet this last point many councils have recently established one-party policy committees as part of their official structure, so that officers can attend and play their part. Sometimes, again, a committee chairman may ask a chief officer for advice which he then reports to his group.

The growth of party politics in local government can be defended mainly on the ground that it leads to consistency in decision-making and enhances the role of the elected member. A non-party system, it is alleged, too easily results in a variety of decisions lacking coherence or consistency; committee recommendations may be overridden after a public debate which is seldom exhaustive and does not enable officers to participate effectively. Under a party system an officer knows where he stands: he makes all his knowledge and experience available to the majority party and, when party policy has been clarified, he then does all he can to make the best of it. Further, because the majority party accepts responsibility for the running of the council it may be prepared to pay more attention to the claims of the finance, establishment, and other horizontal committees than would be paid by a council where there is no party discipline. Coherent council policy replaces a rag-bag of committee or departmental policies.

Though there was little support for the Maud Committee's proposed management board, there was general agreement with most of the other recommendations on committee structures. Indeed several authorities had already reviewed their committee systems before the publication of the report, which frankly sought in part to reflect current best practice. Cheshire County Council, for example, appointed a simplification committee late in 1965, and by 1967 the council had adopted proposals from this committee with major effect on the conduct of county business. Although the result was a suppression of only two main committees (from eighteen to sixteen), the number of subcommittees was reduced from fifty-three to twenty-eight and that of meetings from 398 to 148 a year. In 1966 Bedford Borough Council established a management committee to guide the council's general strategy, its goals, and its priorities. The following year Newcastle-upon-Tyne City Council went some way towards accepting a report from its principal city officer which proposed far more sweeping changes in the committee system than any adopted elsewhere, such as a reduction of main committees from thirty-seven to less than ten and the appointment of two managing committees, for municipal relations and resources planning.

The general reaction to the Maud Report was to review committee structures. A spate of changes took place up and down the country in 1968 and following years, and the average number of committees of county and county borough councils came down from around twenty to a dozen or so. More than half of these councils also adopted some kind of policy committee. Such changes were closely in line with Sir Andrew Wheatley's memorandum of dissent; for committees everywhere retained their executive responsibilities (with the notable exception of one small borough which abolished every committee and decided to conduct all its business in full council).

The aftermath of the report was also marked by increased delegation of council work to committees. With certain important exceptions, such as the power to levy a rate or raise a loan, a council can decide how much to delegate to each committee, and many authorities have for years given committees full power in certain matters: on these a committee does not make recommendations to the council but merely reports what it has done.

In reviewing their committee structure most authorities reconsidered the terms of reference of their committees. As a result many of the larger councils now delegate to committees virtually everything they can, though sometimes with safeguards such as the right of a certain number of committee members to insist that a matter goes to full council for decision.[5] In Cheshire, for example, the reduction in the number of committees and in the frequency of meetings went along with an increase in the work delegated to committees (and in the levels of responsibility delegated to officers, a topic to be explored in the next chapter). County council meetings in consequence take relatively few decisions and for the most part are concerned with reports of action taken by committees. Members may only ask questions about these reports and cannot move 'reference back' or 'non-adoption', a self-denying ordinance which many of them found so hard to bear that the chairman of the council was several times forced to rule members out of order.

THE BAINS REPORT

In the reorganization of London government the new London boroughs were given little advice about their internal organization. They were elected in May 1964, only two months after the Maud Committee was appointed and well before it was able to offer any guidance. No other local authorities in the country were quite like them, for they had fewer powers than county boroughs but many more than county districts. The county borough was the nearest comparable authority and some new London boroughs (Camden, for example) based their first committee and departmental structures on a rapid study of county boroughs of a comparable size.

The Redcliffe-Maud Commission emphasized how important it would be for new councils created in consequence of its report to

[5] The operation of the party system is, of course, another safeguard against committees acting in a manner contrary to the wishes of most members of the council.

avoid the faults of internal organization from which the old councils suffered, and urged that thought be given to this question well in advance of the time when the reformed system became operative. In 1971 the Government and the local authority associations took action to this end. They jointly established a high-powered seven-man working group of clerks and treasurers (together with one industrialist) 'to produce advice for the new local authorities on management structures at both member and officer level'. The group worked under the auspices of a seventeen-member steering committee representative of the main local authority associations. Its report, published in August 1972, became known by the name of its chairman, Mr. M. A. Bains, the Clerk of the Kent County Council.

It may seem that, given the existence of the Maud report, no such exercise was necessary. But there were in fact good reasons for going beyond a reminder to local authorities of the Maud proposals. Especially at elected member level there had been some hostility towards the highly controversial proposals for a management board and non-executive committees, and developments since 1967 were worth investigating. Besides, the new authorities were different from their predecessors.

Since most members of the Bains Committee were senior local government officers, it is not surprising that much of the report reflected current best practice rather than radical ideas. About committee structures it made three main sets of proposals. First, it emphasized the importance of a strong central body which it called the Policy and Resources Committee. This committee was to assist the council in setting objectives and priorities and in co-ordinating and controlling their achievement; it would have three strong subcommittees dealing with the major resources of the authority: finance, manpower, land and buildings. This was a milder version of the suggested management board and was a development of what many counties and county boroughs had by 1970.

Secondly, regarding other committees, Bains clearly favoured a streamlined structure but recognized that 'in a democratic institution management efficiency cannot be the only consideration'. Since elected members both enjoy and demand committee work, each new council should establish a committee structure ensuring that every member serves on at least one committee. Fairly detailed suggestions for committee structures were then made, but only on the understanding that 'there is no "best buy" when it comes to deciding the number of committees which a particular local authority requires'.[6] A firm recommendation followed against creating area committees as executive bodies.

The third set of proposals centred on the idea of a Performance Review Subcommittee (of the policy and resources committee). This idea was new to local government and reflected the experience of the House of Commons Public Accounts Committee.

In emphasizing the need to define objectives and priorities, the report followed the trend of recent years towards 'corporate planning' and 'management by objectives' through such aids as programme planning and budgeting systems. The aim must be to escape from the traditional piecemeal nature of decision-making and establish clear objectives for each service and group of services.

The advantage of this approach is that it makes it possible to measure achievement against expectations. Are resources, once allocated, being properly used? Does the quality of performance suggest that the council's objectives need redefining? Regular monitoring and review procedures should help answer such questions, and the Bains Committee expected each committee to undertake systematic reviews of progress. An additional proposal was that the performances review subcommittee should also be able to investigate in detail any project, department, or area of activity. Its report would be submitted to the policy and resources committee, and the relevant committees and departments would be free to comment on the contents. The membership of this subcommittee would be flexible so that councillors with a particular interest could serve on it during the conduct of perhaps only one investigation.

Like all reports, that of the Bains Committee soon came under fire, especially from two kinds of criticism. First, the committee was said to have paid insufficient attention to the workings of party politics and their impact on decision-making. For example, the report favoured minority party representation on the policy and resources committee, as the Maud Committee had favoured for the management board; and the report further suggested that, if a council adopted bi-partisanship for its central committee, representatives of both majority and minority groups should have access to the officers before the committee meeting. Its arguments in support of these views might well be sound in theory, but they were in practice unacceptable to many authorities which had recently established

---

[6] Department of the Environment, *The New Local Authorities: Management and Structure* (H.M.S.O., 1972), para. 4.38.

one-party policy committees in order to ensure that the majority party had the benefit of professional advice from officers before reaching decisions.

A second criticism was that the report was too dogmatic. It is true that the report includes diagrams of recommended committee and departmental structures for each of the four categories of new authority (metropolitan and non-metropolitan county and the parallel types of district). But such diagrams were given only to illustrate arguments in the text which usually, as in discussing the number of committees, put more than one side of the case. Except for the firm proposal of a policy and resources committee, the recommendations were almost all advanced only as suggestions.

The report certainly influenced most new authorities when they came to discuss committee structures after their election in the spring of 1973. Almost all major authorities—counties of both types and metropolitan districts—decided to draw up programmes for the development of their services over a period of years, based on a statement of objectives, though some were content, like Liverpool and Stockport, to build on already existing programmes. Most councils opted for a committee structure which included a central committee (though not all used the Bains title 'policy and resources'), and the temptation to reproduce old types of structure was resisted. Cheshire County Council, for example, reduced its number of main committees from sixteen to ten, appointed (for the first time) a policy and resources committee, and strove to co-ordinate its work in the environmental field through the creation of a strategic planning and transportation committee. On the other hand the desire of most elected members to serve on at least two committees has often meant the establishment of a structure which on grounds of management efficiency must be judged unwieldly. This has been specially apparent in the metropolitan areas where the large county councils have few major functions. The Greater Manchester County Council, for example, has ten committees and, so that every councillor may serve on two, the membership of each committee is twenty-one. Three horizontal committees are responsible for policy, finance, and personnel, and there are service committees for planning, highways, transportation, police, fire, consumer protection, and recreation.

A restructuring of the areas of local government requires a major Act of Parliament: this results in clear landmarks such as 1963 for

London and 1972 for the rest of England; and each act caused a major upheaval throughout the affected area. But changes in the internal organization of local government cannot be charted in this way. The Maud and Bains Reports of 1967 and 1972 preface or mark the climax of a period of transition. They may affect the character of subsequent developments, but their influence over the pattern of events is far less clear than that of legislation.

However, between, say, 1958 and 1974 not only the national framework of English local government but its inner working undoubtedly went through a period of major change. At the end of the 1950s most local councils were organizing their work in ways which would have been instantly recognizable to people such as Joseph Redlich who were writing about English local government at the turn of the century. As services came and went the names of the various committees changed but the principle which underlay their appointment did not. The inner structure of councils was dominated by vertical committees. Members were spending their time in committee meetings and were taking decisions, at least in a formal sense, on a huge number of heterogeneous detailed questions, some of them of great moment, involving large sums of money and much personal happiness or suffering, some of them utterly trivial.

Recent developments in council organization have had three main effects on the work of the councillor. First, fewer matters of detail now go to committee for decision: councils delegate more responsibility to their officers. Such delegation has always been necessary, for councillors could never allocate all children to secondary schools or negotiate with each of their contractors. But only recently has the legal situation been so clarified that authorities can now specifically delegate responsibility for parts of services to officers: the 1972 act explicitly gave them this power, generalizing a clause in the 1968 Town and Country Planning Act which related only to the one service.

Secondly, new emphasis has been placed on the need for a corporate approach to be made by each council to its whole span of work. Part of the general case for local government is that it can co-ordinate the provision of various local services and decide priorities on behalf of the whole local community. But the natural tendency of some chief officers to put their professional interest in a particular service before the general interest of society meant that councils frequently lacked a balanced approach to the competing claims on their resources. The general use of vertical committees gave many chief officers a strong ally in their committee chairman, and the result was often more like a series of semi-independent service-providing agencies than one coherent local council. Horizontal committees were frequently weak—even the strongest of them, the finance committee, often reacted only negatively to the estimates of service departments, without seeking to recommend an integrated set of priorities for the council to consider. Many developments of the past decade have been aimed at so strengthening horizontal committees and rationalizing the structure of vertical committees that attention can be focused on the work of the council as a whole, not only on individual services, and that the needs of the community can thus be judged in fair perspective. The average member now serves on rather fewer committees than in earlier days. He may feel frustrated when told that 'the policy committee will not agree'. But he may succeed eventually in influencing that committee through private meetings of his party group.

The third effect, closely linked to the second, has been a strengthening of the elected member in his relations with the officers. Comparatively few authorities used to have strong or consistent leadership from councillors. But the development of the concept of management by objectives has encouraged councils to clarify their immediate and longer term priorities. The growth of policy committees has put elected members in a stronger position to play their crucial part in this process of self-examination. The committee chairman has become a still more important link between the officers and the party, and the back-bench councillor must now work more closely with his party if he is to influence major decisions. The minority party member finds it increasingly difficult to initiate change. In all these ways local government has come perceptibly closer to the parliamentary model, with its clear distinction between the functions of government and opposition and between those of front-bench and back-bench member.

7
Officers

THERE are three reasons why local government cannot be carried on without the help of paid officers. First, there is ignorance. Local government requires a professional and technical knowledge of the law, accountancy, education, town planning, engineering, architecture, and many other social and natural sciences. Councillors cannot be expected to know much about detailed matters such as these: they therefore require the help and advice of paid experts. The elected member concerns himself more with the human side of local services: his experience is indispensable if the experts are to be kept informed of what the public will and will not stand and are to be controlled accordingly.

The second reason is the possible corruptibility of elected members. They are not in the habit of accepting bribes in the simple sense of the word. But they have offered themselves as candidates for a variety of reasons; they owe their success in the election to a variety of people; and much of the work of a local council offers a variety of temptations. However stringently the law and local authorities forbid councillors to speak or vote on matters in which they have a financial interest, many temptations will remain. But some of them are removed, and some made less alluring, by the appointment of full-time officials whose business it is to remain apart from all local 'interests', whether political or of any other kind.

Thirdly there is lack of leisure. Elected members are unpaid, and very few can give their whole time to local government. But the administration of important services must be continuous, and there is no alternative to the appointment of persons to remain on duty between meetings and implement council decisions. Furthermore, some local authorities are very large undertakings and several thousand councillors would be needed for each area if they were to perform the work of the authority.

In 1973 more than $2\frac{1}{4}$ million people, or nearly 10 per cent of the working population of England, were employed by local authorities —a figure which reflects the range of services provided by county and district councils. Other figures show how high a proportion of local government expenditure goes to meet the salary and wages bill. For example, more than half of the annual expenditure on education, libraries, museums, and art galleries, the police and fire services, parks, public health, and the social services is paid out as wages or salaries to staff.[1]

THE LOCAL GOVERNMENT SERVICE

Yet despite the importance of local government as a source of employment there is no one local government service. The service is fragmented both between local authorities and within each of them. Nationally there is no central control over establishments nor is there a single employing body: each council recruits and selects its own officers. Even within a single authority each of the various departments often undertakes its own recruitment, certainly of junior officers, though the degree of co-ordination and control varies widely from one council to another.

Numerous related developments have in recent decades much reduced this fragmentation but it remains an important feature of the English local government service. Officers are still employed by individual authorities and, though they often choose to move in the course of a career from one employer to another, they cannot be posted from place to place. But the salaries paid by different councils are much less varied than they used to be. Similarly, the terms and conditions of service on which officers are employed have largely become standardized though local variation remains. These changes have resulted from the gradual growth of national negotiating machinery and of a national training organization.

Several kinds of national negotiating machinery are at work today. For administrative workers there is the National Joint

[1] Department of the Environment, *Local Government Financial Statistics 1971–72* (H.M.S.O., 1973), p. 48.

Council for Local Authorities' Administrative, Professional, Technical and Clerical Services. Founded in 1943, this council of some sixty members, half of whom speak for the local authorities and half for the employees (represented through unions like NALGO, the National and Local Government Officers Association), has negotiated salary increases and produced standard conditions of service. The salary of teachers is negotiated nationally by another body, the Burnham Committee, established in 1920 and consisting of a similar proportion of members representing employers and the several unions. Manual workers are represented by trades unions such as the Transport and General Workers, the National Union of General and Municipal Workers, and the National Union of Public Employees. Other national organizations include the Fire Brigade's Union and the Police Federation.

The training of officers has also been partially integrated on a national basis and since 1946 a Local Government Examinations Board has been specially concerned with the training of clerical and administrative staff. In consequence of two developments in the mid-1960s the board changed its name and broadened its role: it is now known as the Local Government Training Board (L.G.T.B.). These changes followed the passage by Parliament of the Industrial Training Act of 1964 (which increased the national emphasis on training and introduced a system of levies and grants, operated by more than two dozen training boards for different industries) and the recommendations of the Mallaby Committee on the Staffing of Local Government in 1967.

Fragmentation of staffing within the local authority has also been reduced, though each council organizes its internal affairs much as it likes. A major development followed the strong recommendation of the Bains Report that local authorities should pay much more attention to staff management. A whole chapter was devoted to this subject, encouraging councils to improve their methods of staff selection and manpower planning, and to further the education, training, and career development of their officers. The report suggested the appointment of a personnel officer with direct access to the council's chief executive and with a status which would encourage other chief officers to accept his advice. The traditional establishment officer usually handled a much narrower range of duties, such as the administration of rules on pay and conditions, disciplinary action, and preliminary negotiations with the unions: he was seldom able to develop policies for recruitment and, more rarely still, for training (often the responsibility of a quite separate training officer).

Fragmentation of the service posed a specially difficult problem during the reorganization period—1964–5 in London and 1973–4 elsewhere. The importance of maintaining staff morale and performance during the period was fully recognized. At both times a similar solution was adopted: the appointment of a Local Government Staff Commission to safeguard the interests of the staff. The commissions themselves could not issue directives to local authorities though they could advise the Minister to do so. Instead they worked through circulars and gave advice which they expected local authorities to follow. This covered such matters as the handling of new appointments during the months immediately preceding reorganization, advising staff of their future post in the new authority, and methods of appointment of chief and senior officers. Both commissions recommended that as many of such appointments as possible should be made locally and asked the new councils to recruit from outside their area only in cases of real necessity (for example, a new metropolitan district or London borough which was not based on a county borough had no obvious candidates for senior posts in the education or social services departments, as this work had previously been done by county, not district councils). One important exception to this general advice concerned the appointment by the new county and metropolitan district councils in 1973 of their chief executives. For these posts the Staff Commission issued advertisements on a national basis; any serving local government officer, apart from those in London, could apply.

The problem arising from fragmentation was also recognized by Parliament in two other ways during debates on the Local Government Act of 1972. First, all employees were guaranteed new terms and conditions of service not less favourable than their existing ones, unless they were either made redundant or assigned new duties less demanding than the old. Staff in London received similar treatment a decade earlier. Secondly, during the final months before reorganization local councils could upgrade staff only in certain circumstances, and these were defined by a joint body known as the Local Authorities (Conditions of Service) Advisory Board. This latter restriction had not applied during the London reorganization, but was included in the 1972 act following evidence (submitted to the Redcliffe-Maud Commission) that in London some old authorities had upgraded large numbers of officers in order to improve their

prospects under the new. One metropolitan borough upgraded 97
per cent of its employees; Middlesex County Council attempted to
award pay increases for all grades.[2]

Thanks partly to the Staff Commissions and still more to the good
relations generally existing between councillors and staff in local
government, reorganization in London and the rest of England
passed off smoothly. The public continued to receive services and,
as elections to the new authorities were held a year before the date
of the transfer of power, few citizens were even aware of the over-
night change in responsibilities on 1 April 1965 and 1974. In 1965
throughout the whole of Greater London only 172 officers were
made redundant and an elaborate appeals machinery set up by the
Staff Commission to hear objections to proposed transfers of officers
was used only thirty-eight times.[3]

THE OFFICER'S FUNCTION

Relations between a local government officer and the council
contrast sharply with those between a national civil servant and
Parliament. The latter are not the servants of Parliament but of the
Crown. It is the Crown (on the Prime Minister's advice), and not
Parliament, that appoints the Minister who temporarily heads a
government department and the civil servants who form its permanent staff. Though by convention the Minister directs the policy
of his department in accordance with the wishes of Parliament and
has to answer in Parliament for the work of his department, the
relationship is not that of servant to master. Local government
officers on the other hand are servants of the local council and
derive from it their powers and duties.

All the actions of the local government officer are performed in
the name of the council. But in practice not all matters are discussed by the councillors, either in full council or in committee or
subcommittee. Responsibility for implementing council policy is
delegated to the officer and he will only bring a matter to the
attention of a committee when it is of some importance or when
the course of action which he should take is not clear.

Traditionally local authorities have organized themselves in a

---

[2] G. Rhodes, *The Government of London: the struggle for reform* (Weidenfeld &
Nicolson, 1970), pp. 219–20.

[3] See *Report of the London Government Staff Commission* (H.M.S.O., 1966). The
commission had estimated that there would be between 500 and 1,000 appeals.

series of departments, each with responsibility for a particular service. Most departments provide services direct to the public—education, social services, libraries, parks. Others support these service departments from inside the organization, their work being common to all or several services—the clerk's, treasurer's, or architect's department for example. The parallel with the traditional committee structure outlined earlier is clear enough: service departments correspond to the vertical committees, support departments to the horizontal.

An important feature of this internal organization has been the dominance of professionally qualified officers in the top posts. A social services department, for example, is headed by a director of social services, one or two deputy directors and up to about five assistant directors, all of whom are trained social workers. Professional qualifications are therefore an essential condition of career progress, and the administrator who lacks them, commonly known as a lay administrative officer, cannot find his way into top departmental posts.

A further result of this professionalism is that, while administrative officers may on occasion trasnfer from one department to another, internal mobility among senior staff is rare, indeed nearly impossible. Even among more junior staff it is uncommon: more than 75 per cent of authorities replying to a questionnaire from the Mallaby Committee reported that they made no arrangements enabling selected officers to widen their experience in this way. Here is a striking contrast to the tradition of the national civil service where mobility of staff at all levels has been common and, until recently, 'generalists' have held the senior positions. The chief reason for the contrast lies in the nature of local government services. In general there has been a larger professional or technical content in the day-to-day work of a local authority than in that of most central departments and this has led to the employment of officers with high technical and professional qualifications in the top positions.

One result has been that a local authority has tended in the past to be a collection of departments, each providing a single service. Yet a council elected to govern its local community ought by its very nature to take a comprehensive view of the services needed and seek to provide what it considers to be the right mixture of those services. There should therefore be a balance between the professional freedom accorded to service departments and the central co-ordination of policy-making and resource allocation. It is the achievement of this balance that has been at the heart of the discussion in recent years about organization structures and has led the majority of the new councils to create some such central machinery as a policy and resources committee.

THE CHIEF EXECUTIVE

The arguments about departmental structures have been similar to those that have led to a strengthening of horizontal committees. They have centred on the role of the town clerk or clerk to the council. All the committees of inquiry (Maud, Mallaby, and Bains) have unanimously recommended that he be given a stronger position, with clear authority over all the departmental heads. Both the Mallaby and Bains Reports suggested that he should be called Chief Executive in order to make this plain.

In practice council clerks have for years been the most influential officers in many authorities, and they have usually been lawyers. Their function has been to give legal advice both to elected members and to other officers, provide secretarial services for the council and its committees, and handle relations with other authorities, outside bodies, and central government. Such work clearly places the clerk in a powerful position: he is the centre of a communications network which relates him to all aspects of council business and gives him access to a breadth of knowledge which departmental heads and elected members lack. Once appointed he is virtually irremovable. His influence can be greater than any of his professional colleagues or indeed than any member of the council.

Given this background, the proposal for the creation of a chief executive as the acknowleged leader of a team of officers and with authority over the whole paid staff of the council may not seem radical. By force of personality many clerks have in the past done precisely what the Mallaby and Bains Committees said a chief executive should do. The main difference is that these tasks are now stated explicitly. For example, on the advice of professional management consultants, the following job description for a chief executive and town clerk was adopted by the Liverpool City Council in 1970:

The Chief Executive and Town Clerk is the head of the Corporation's paid service. He provides the necessary information and co-ordinated staff services to the City Council through the Policy and Finance Committee in matters of policy, and in the adoption of plans and priorities for the provision of services and the development of the City. He ensures that the Council's approved policies and plans are effectively implemented, by controlling and co-ordinating the Corporation's organisation and resources so that the agreed mix and level of services are provided as economically as possible. In addition, he represents and negotiates on behalf of the Council with outside agencies and individuals whose activities affect the City and its people.

Such a statement emphasizes the centrality of the chief executive in the organizational structure and his formal responsibility for the efficient working of the council and its staff of 45,000. Even so, he differs fundamentally from an American city manager: for example, he has no powers to 'hire and fire' senior members of the staff.

The concept of a chief executive has been widely accepted in local government in the last few years. The restatement of the general arguments in the Bains Report in 1972 provoked little dissent.[4] There has been wide support for the idea of corporate planning of the whole work of a council, enabling it to formulate objectives in advance, decide between alternative methods of achieving them, measure performance against programme, and meet the need for stronger central management than could be guaranteed by following traditional ways. Some controversy, however, arose over the suggestion that the chief executive, in order to be free from day-to-day routine responsibility, should not be head of a department. The legal and committee work of the council would come under a more traditional clerk (the report preferred the title 'secretary'), while the chief executive would only have a small staff of two or three personal assistants of his own, mainly concerned with research, policies, and programmes.

While the majority of the larger councils, the counties and metropolitan districts, opted for a non-departmental chief executive in 1973, a substantial minority did not. These took the view that the advantages for the chief executive of being at the centre of the council's regular communications network outweighed any disadvantages of concern with daily routine. Five counties used the designation 'Clerk and Chief Executive' for their senior officer; others, like Cheshire, made it clear in their advertisements for a county secretary that he would be working within the chief executive's department.

---

[4] Liverpool's job description may be compared with that proposed by the Bains Committee. The latter is longer but gives the chief executive similar duties: see *Bains Report*, Appendix, 5, p. 165.

Recent debate, then, about the work of local government officers has concentrated on management and planning. This tendency has been generally apparent throughout industry and commerce, and also in discussion of reform in public corporations and the civil service. Its special significance for local government has been to emphasize the need for managerial ability in the training and selection of chief officers and to challenge traditional assumptions about the overriding importance of technical or professional qualifications. The Maud, Mallaby, and Bains Reports all agreed that the post of chief executive is one which requires managerial ability rather than professional or technical expertise. But none of them suggested that the same applied to departmental heads.

The Mallaby Report envisaged far better career prospects for the lay administrative officer in future as the proportion of administrative work in a council's larger departments grew, and it recommended advanced training for the more promising administrator. But it did not go so far as to recommend that such officers should be eligible for the headship of a department: it suggested only that the second or third post in a departmental hierarchy might be open to him. The post of chief executive, on the other hand, was considered to be exceptional: this officer would have to deal with 'high administrative tasks requiring distinctive gifts of personality and leadership', and these gifts a generalist officer was as likely to possess as a member of one of the professions. The Maud and Bains Committees concurred in this analysis.

It was in the field of the clerk or chief executive that a few experimental top-level appointments were made before 1973. In 1965, for example, a senior executive of the Ford Motor Company, Mr. Frank Harris, was appointed 'Principal City Officer with Town Clerk' by Newcastle-upon-Tyne city council, but he remained only a few years in office and his appointment was quite exceptional. Indeed, the appointment from within local government of a chief executive who is not a qualified lawyer has hitherto been rare: a professional local government treasurer has been appointed by Brighton, Coventry, Oxford, and some other councils, a planner by East Suffolk County Council. In one or two smaller districts, where the functions of the council are much more limited than those of counties or county boroughs, an engineer or surveyor has occasionally been appointed chief executive. In 1973 county and metropolitan district councils were allowed by the Staff Commission to appoint any serving local government officer as chief executive.

Many who were not clerks—treasurers and planning officers in particular—applied. But the new councils made few experiments. Only one county failed to appoint a serving clerk or deputy clerk: Cleveland chose the treasurer of Teesside, the county borough which dominated the new county. The metropolitan districts were a little more adventurous: Stockport and Doncaster appointed treasurers, for example, and Birmingham chose Liverpool's planning officer.

THE CORPORATE APPROACH

In emphasizing the corporate nature of a local authority's work, the Bains Report recommended the formal recognition of an officers management team led by the chief executive in the council's organization. It argued that 'it is of the essence of the corporate approach to management that chief officers recognize that there are few if any major decisions which can be made in isolation without some impact upon others' areas of responsibility',[5] and it saw the team as being the counterpart, at officer level, of the policy and resources committee.

This was no new concept in 1972. Many authorities had for some years held regular meetings of chief officers under the chairmanship of the clerk. Cheshire County Council, for example, developed such a system in the 1960s: there the main chief officers met regularly five or six times a year from 1968, and less regularly in the earlier part of the decade. The chief officers board appointed working parties to study and report back on such matters as personnel selection, management development, and purchasing policies, while more permanent steering committees were used to review the use of the computer, transport co-ordination, and subsidies to rural bus routes. At the level of chief administrative officer (that is, the most senior of such posts) a parallel series of meetings under the chairmanship of the senior assistant in the clerk's department was also begun. In the London Borough of Hammersmith, created in 1965, the town clerk's co-ordinating committee met even more frequently; by early 1967 meetings were being held every week, though later this was modified to a fortnightly cycle.

One difficulty in establishing such a management team is to decide on its composition. If all heads of department are to be members this can result in too large a body in many authorities: a county council might have a dozen or more departmental heads,

[5] *Report*, para. 5.40.

and a county borough (under the pre-1974 structure) anything from fifteen to thirty separate departments.[6] It is questionable whether a team as large as twelve or more can operate with real efficiency.

Three solutions to this problem are commonly being sought, sometimes simultaneously. First, not all chief officers need to be permanent members. Provided that they receive reports of the meetings and are invited to attend when something which clearly affects them is on the agenda, heads of small departments can be excluded from membership. In Cheshire, for example, the land agent and valuer is not normally invited to attend meetings. The Bains Report suggested that in a metropolitan district the management team might possibly exclude the architect, engineer, librarian, and several other heads of small departments.

Secondly, departments can be grouped under a small number of directors. The Bains Report suggested, as a second alternative for a metropolitan district, the appointment of six directors: four for traditional departments, another for educational services who would be overlord of the education, libraries, and recreation departments, and another for technical services who would cover the interests of estates, planning, architects, engineers, and environmental health departments. A modified form of this approach was adopted in Hammersmith, where the town clerk's co-ordinating committee consisted of the clerk, treasurer, architect and planning officer, engineer and medical officer of health. Officers such as the housing manager and estates valuer were indirectly represented through the clerk, the welfare and children's officers through the medical officer. In 1973 Cheshire County Council decided to establish a strategic planning and transportation management board, to supplement its chief officers' board by concerning itself solely with the plans and policies of the architect's, planner's, surveyor's, and land agent's departments. The chief executive acts as chairman. The board reports to the strategic planning and transportation committee mentioned in Chapter 6. Both Hammersmith and Cheshire adopted the more modern title of Director for several of their chief officers in the late 1960s.

[6] The new town clerk of Nottingham found twenty-eight on his appointment in 1966. Four of these were headed by engineers: the City Engineer, the Lighting Engineer, the Water Engineer, and the City Sewage-Disposal Engineer. Royal Institute of Public Administration, *Management of Local Government: Report of a Conference 12–13th December 1967* (R.I.P.A., 1968), p. 59.

The third solution, recommended by the Maud Committee, seems the most simple: to create a management structure based on only half a dozen or so departments and chief officers, through the merging of small departments combined with the use of overlords.

The amalgamation of smaller departments has occurred in many places in addition to that enforced by the Local Authority Social Services Act of 1970 which merged welfare and children's departments. But for two reasons amalgamations have been less popular than departmental grouping under an overlord. First, some chief officers must be appointed by law and their departments are virtually certain to remain distinct. Under the 1972 Local Government Act, the relevant authorities must appoint chief education officers, fire officers, and directors of social services. The chief constable is also a statutory appointment. Before 1972 the list was much more extensive, including clerks, treasurers, medical officers of health, and (in boroughs and urban districts) surveyors. Secondly, local government officers come from a wide variety of professions. Although the work of architect, planning officer, surveyor, and housing manager may be closely linked, each office has its own professional and technical content. Members of these professions entering the local government service have traditionally had the prospect of a career structure leading to chief officer status. They naturally attach importance to such prospects, nor will authorities endanger staff morale by taking the drastic steps that might be taken on grounds of efficiency alone. Nor do committee chairmen always relish a radical amalgamation of departments.

The concept of corporate planning has usually won the support of leading elected members in councils organized on strictly party lines. The new approach enhances their power and influence, as well as giving added emphasis to the council's central departments. Some committee chairmen may not be happy at the prospect of less freedom for their committee, but the appointment of all committee chairmen to a new policy committee has often secured their support. Clerks and treasurers normally welcome the emphasis on central co-ordination and a rationalized system of resource allocation, but some heads of spending departments have been less easy to win over, and many councils have employed outside management consultants as much to justify reforms as to obtain new ideas for increased effectiveness. The main firms of consultants have between them reviewed hundreds of authorities in recent years and have almost invariably advised the adoption of corporate planning and stronger central management. Their detailed recommendations have been peculiar to the council under review, but their general line of approach has been more widely applicable. Such reports have provided valuable independent support for those councillors and officers who are anxious to improve their existing organization.

Training in management for senior officers has also developed, particularly at the University of Birmingham's Institute of Local Government Studies. Lengthy residential courses, designed to teach management techniques and their application to local authority work, were at first open to clerks only. Later, heads of other departments, their deputies and other senior officers became eligible. Several hundred senior officers have now attended courses there or have had management training at other similar institutions. This contrasts sharply with the traditional local government attitude that officers received this kind of training only 'on the job'.

Most local councils today have a quite different organizational structure, at both councillor and officer levels, from that which dominated local government until the 1960s. Today more emphasis is placed on the comprehensive planning of services and on leadership from the council's centre. In consequence most authorities have established a central committee and a chief executive with formal responsibility for the oversight of the activities of spending committees and departmental heads. The working of party politics further strengthens the role of the central committee in almost all urban and most county authorities. The chief executive's role has been strengthened by the increased acceptance among other chief officers of the value of corporate planning and management and by the rapid growth of management services: work study, organization and methods, operational research, network analysis, cost–benefit analysis, programme planning and budgeting, and other newer techniques, sometimes directed comprehensively by a management services unit within the chief executive's department. Successful partnership between the leader of the council (or senior politician of the majority party) and the chief executive has become a significant objective.

The relationship between elected members and officers, however, is not always easy. It has been under constant strain for many years, indeed ever since council services began to expand and become more scientific and sophisticated. Expansion has forced the elected member to relax his control over the details of service provision, for

he remains a part-time politician. Scientific and technical developments have made it increasingly difficult for him to make informed
judgements about complex problems, for he is an untrained
generalist. He has to develop his own methods of work if he is to
retain effective control. In theory officers are the servants of the
council. In practice the distinction between master and servant
cannot be clear-cut.

The difficulty of distinguishing between the proper functions of
councillor and officer is not removed by calling the member's
function 'policy' and the officer's 'administration'. The Maud
Committee pointed out that a succession of administrative decisions
can contribute eventually to the formulation of policy. The Bains
Report was inclined to support the view that the management process
'can be seen as a scale, with the setting of objectives and allocation
of major resources at one end, moving through the designing of
programmes and plans, to the execution of those plans at the other
end. As one moves through that management scale, the balance
between the two elements changes from member control with
officer advice at the "objective" end to officer control with member
advice at the "execution" end'. Much depends in practice on the
attitudes and personalities of the people concerned, and emphasis is
rightly placed in all these reports on such phrases as 'the need for
mutual trust and understanding' and 'working in partnership
towards a common end'. Rightly, too, all the reports acknowledge
that frequently such ideals prove unattainable. As the Bains
Committee put it: 'elected members and officers (are) too often
suspicious and critical of each other's role, and although friction and
competition may aid efficiency they have in some authorities been
allowed to impair both morale and efficiency'.[8] Not only do local
authorities vary widely in the structure of their internal organization, they also behave in very different ways.

[7] *Report*, paras. 3.14–15.   [8] *Report*, para. 2.6.

8
Finance

THE subject of local government finance contains one of the chief clues in answering the question how far local councils are genuine organs of self-government. In 1971–2 English local authorities spent around £8,500 million,[1] or more than five times the total sales of the giant Industrial Chemical Industries Ltd. (I.C.I.). Six years earlier the figure was only half as great, and the gravity of many present problems of local finance is due to the speed at which expenditure has grown. The rate of increase (except for the part caused by depreciation of the pound) reflects the developing importance of local government's services: education, the social services, leisure and amenity provision have become major growth points in the national economy and councils now incur one-third of all public expenditure, a proportion which is expected to increase steadily.

Another mark of the importance of local expenditure is the proportion of gross national product (G.N.P.) for which it accounts. G.N.P. is in effect the total sum, in money terms, of the economic activity of the whole country in a year. At the turn of the century, local government's proportion was around 5 per cent. Today the percentage is more than 16, and this rise has further quickened the national interest in local action. British governments today accept general responsibility for the national economy and clearly they cannot allow such a large part of it to go free. So they are bound to seek, by controlling capital expenditure undertaken locally and supplementing local revenue by grants-in-aid, to exercise a great influence on local spending.

[1] Department of the Environment, *Local Government Financial Statistics 1971–2* (H.M.S.O., 1973).

The distinction made here between capital and revenue expenditure is an important feature of local government financial practice. Where a local authority spends money on something which will serve the area for many years it finances the project from its capital account. New schools, libraries, roads, and housing estates are common instances. Where money is being spent on something which is valuable only in the short term, payment is made from its revenue account: salaries of staff are the most important example. Capital and revenue accounts are brought together in the repayment and interest charges made each year for loans raised, say, for the building of a school. As with salary payments, the short-term value of the school is reflected in this expenditure from the revenue account. Only for very old schools, libraries, and other buildings are there no loan charges, for here the original loan has been paid off in full. The whole process, and the distinction between capital and revenue finance, is in essence no different from the experience of an individual who obtains a mortgage for a house or accepts hire-purchase commitments. The expenditure figure of £8,500 million, quoted earlier, includes both capital and revenue outlays.

Capital expenditure then is financed largely through loans. Revenue expenditure is financed in three different ways. Government grants meet a large proportion (about 40 per cent), local rates a slightly smaller one (about 30 per cent), and local income from fees, bus fares, rents of council houses, and other payments charged by the council for a particular service accounts for the remaining 30 per cent.

Before these sources of income are reviewed, there are three general points to be made. First, local authorities have only one local tax of their own—the rates. They can make minor changes in their charges for services (bus fares, for instance), but these have relatively little effect on their total income, especially since 1972 when the Housing Finance Act reduced their power to decide locally the rents of council houses. In effect, local authority freedom to raise income is limited to their rating power, nor is it easy in practice for a council to increase its income dramatically by that means.

Secondly, local authority accounts are subject to audit control. The accounts of each authority are audited annually by an independent external auditor. As many of the larger authorities supplement this by regular permanent internal audit, financial malpractices on any appreciable scale are most unlikely.

Finally, the whole question of local government finance has been under continuous review in recent years. The outcome has been most disappointing to those who hoped for radical changes such as the creation of new local taxes or the transfer to local government of taxes at present monopolized by central government.

CAPITAL FINANCE

In 1971–2 local authorities spent £960m. on building houses, just under £300m. on new schools and colleges, £230m. on roads, and the same amount on water and sewerage services. These together account for the bulk of the £2,100m. spent on capital account: the only other services on which more than £30m. was spent were planning and the social services.[2]

Not all this money was raised through loans. A little over £110m. came from government grants. Almost all such grants are made towards revenue expenditure, but a major exception is for capital spent on highways (in 1971–2 these grants amounted to £95m.), and minor sums relate to sewerage and land drainage.[3] Local revenue contributed a slightly smaller total, for some councils finance small capital projects (such as public conveniences or branch libraries) without raising a loan by using part of their regular income from rates, fees, and grants.

Loans are raised in various ways. The government-sponsored Public Works Loan Board (P.W.L.B.) has been a major source for many years (it celebrates its centenary in 1975), though central government has restricted local access to it from time to time. Bonds, mortgages, and stock issues are also popular methods of raising loans; the reader of almost any newspaper, local or national, may see advertisements from individual local authorities offering attractive rates of interest on money loaned for anything from one to three years.[4] The biggest councils often issue stock which can be bought or sold on the stock exchange at prices quoted daily on the city page of major newspapers. From 1969 more than twenty large authorities, including Derbyshire, Manchester, Birmingham, and Coventry,

---

[2] A full breakdown of expenditure, capital, and revenue, between services is in Appendix 2, p. 171.

[3] The capital grant for highways was replaced in 1974 by a new grant-in-aid towards all transportation functions. This is a cross between a capital and a revenue grant.

[4] A more detailed description of the techniques of local government financial operations is to be found in N. P. Hepworth, *The Finance of Local Government* (Allen & Unwin, 1970).

obtained powers under local Acts of Parliament to borrow from abroad: the 1972 act extended these powers to all councils and in 1973 the Chancellor of the Exchequer encouraged larger ones to seek foreign loans. Smaller authorities rely more on bonds and on the P.W.L.B.

But councils are much less free to decide how much to borrow: they need loan sanction before incurring capital expenditure. Today this is a major method by which central government controls local government's share of public investment and it is used as a national economic regulator. Historically the technique developed for rather different reasons. In the nineteenth century there were few professionally qualified local government officials and loan sanction was a way of ensuring that central departments could check the detailed plans for, say, new sewers or a Poor Law workshop. It was also a device for preventing local authorities from undertaking obligations beyond their means. Some authorities at that time avoided loan sanction through private legislation, but this has become rare since the turn of the century. The London County Council always remained an exception, having secured the right to promote in Parliament an annual bill which gave it power to borrow up to a specified total limit: the Greater London Council inherited this power. The limit is negotiated in private meetings between the council and the relevant government departments, so that the figure appearing in the bill normally reflects an agreement reached before the parliamentary process has begun.

Until 1970 loan sanction was coupled with project approval. A council wishing to build, say, a new library had to apply to the Department of Education and Science for approval of its plans, and to the Ministry of Housing and Local Government for loan sanction (as the latter department dealt with all loan sanctions except for public transport, for which the Ministry of Transport was responsible).[5] The Ministry of Housing would issue the loan sanction only when it learnt from the Department of Education that the plans were satisfactory, that the cost would fall within the total allocated by the treasury for new library buildings, and that the department was content to allow the library to be built. Thus the approval of the Department of Education was more crucial than the issue of loan sanction by the Ministry of Housing.

Since 1970 a new system of loan sanction has been in operation.

[5] In 1970 the two ministries were merged in the new Department of the Environment.

The object has been to reduce the amount of detailed central control over capital expenditure and so give the local council greater freedom. Local authorities now receive an annual block loan sanction and therefore know in advance how much they can spend on capital projects. However, for projects which come under what are described as key-sector services, detailed project approval from the relevant central department remains necessary. This key sector includes the bulk of projects undertaken by education, housing, and social service authorities, and accounts for some three-quarters of the block sanction. The remaining one-quarter consists of locally determined schemes such as for arts, sport, recreation, libraries, town centre development, town halls, or public conveniences.[6]

The effect of this new approach can be summarized as follows. First, local authorities still cannot exceed a prescribed level of total capital expenditure and central government therefore retains its power to alter the rate of capital investment. Secondly, small capital projects no longer have to be individually approved. So long as they can be financed within the authority's block allocation for locally determined schemes, they can be undertaken at the council's discretion. Thus an authority can decide on its own priorities among these projects: it may use all its allocation to build libraries or all of it to build conveniences if that is what it wants. Thirdly, for major projects, such as new schools and housing estates, the new system makes much less difference. The council still has to persuade the relevant ministry to give it project approval, and this has for years been the important hurdle to negotiate. Finally, the block sanction for locally determined schemes is made to county councils and divided, after local consultation and agreement, between the county and the district and parish councils. Continuous liaison between councils is therefore necessary and is usually undertaken by a joint committee and a working party of treasurers.

Those who have argued for local authority freedom over capital expenditure have been disappointed by the 1970 changes. Most would agree that central government must retain its final power to control the over-all level of this expenditure. Some argue that within its total allocation a council should be allowed to choose its own priorities: in other words, the locally determined part of the block-loan sanction should cover all capital projects and not a mere

[6] Details of the scheme are contained in Department of the Environment, *Capital Programmes*, Circular 2/70 (H.M.S.O., 1970). Minor modifications made subsequently do not affect the main principles.

quarter of them. Such an argument, however, takes little account of the real world of politics. National politicians are as concerned with the development of major public services—education, roads, housing, and the like—as are the local councillors. Parliamentary elections are fought on these issues and ministers are responsible for departments which seek to implement national policies through local government. No minister of education, for example, is prepared to lose the power to control investment in new schools. Indeed, no government can disinterest itself in the spread of investment between major services. Nor would public opinion tolerate such abdication of responsibility.

In this political situation the 1970 changes are as much as can be expected. They certainly give councils greater freedom to shape the development of their services. The balance between key-sector and locally determined schemes can of course be amended (it has been marginally changed each year), but complete local flexibility remains a quite unrealistic aim.

REVENUE ACCOUNT

Twenty per cent of revenue expenditure, or more than £1,200m. per year out of a total (in 1971–2) of £6,250m., goes to repay loans. Having accepted a firm commitment when raising the loan, a council has no control over the amount to be repaid each year. Nor in practice has it total control over the remaining 80 per cent of its revenue budget, as most of this is needed for the salaries of staff and much of the rest for other costs associated with their employment: office furniture, lighting, heating, stationery, telephones, and so on. As local government officers have substantial security of tenure, a council seeking to prune its estimates in any year may find itself with comparatively little room for manoeuvre. Taking out every other light bulb in the town hall corridors, as one authority did a few years ago, may be one of its few options.

Whereas the capital expenditure of local government has been dominated by housing, which has accounted for about half the total, its revenue expenditure is dominated by education. In 1971–2 local education authorities spent £2,350m.—or almost 40 per cent of all revenue expenditure by local councils.[7] If housing and the trading services (water, buses, harbours) are excluded, since they

[7] A breakdown of revenue expenditure on each major service is in Appendix 2, p. 171.

were largely financed out of rents and income from fees charged to individual users, then education accounted that year for virtually half of local government's revenue expenditure. This was six times the proportion of the next most expensive services, police and roads, and eight times that of local authority social services.

As to individual charges, council house tenants paid nearly £550 million in rents, passengers on municipal buses (excluding those controlled by the passenger transport authorities in the conurbations) £65m. in fares, users of civic restaurants nearly £3m. Many trading services are self-balancing and some even make a profit, which is used to pay for other services and so keep down the rates. Manchester, for example makes a yearly profit of some half a million pounds from Ringway Airport.

Most local services, however, are provided free of charge or are heavily subsidized. Education departments, for example, collected less than £225m. in fees (from people attending evening classes, payments for school dinners, etc.) and this did not go far to offset an expenditure of £2,350m. The major part of local government expenditure is therefore met by payments from two groups of citizen, taxpayers and ratepayers. Many are members of both groups, some only of one.

All general taxpayers contribute to local expenditure but only indirectly, through central government grants-in-aid. Over the years the method of calculating and distributing these grants has varied, with a post-war trend towards block payments instead of the previously popular specific grants. In 1973 forty-seven specific grants still remained,[8] but they accounted in total for only 10 per cent of government aid. Further, with the progressive reduction of housing subsidies under the Housing Finance Act of 1972, they are declining rapidly in importance and under legislation in 1974 more of them have been replaced. The grant of 50 per cent of approved expenditure by local police authorities—£180m. in 1971–2—is the largest of those that remain.

An exception to the trend towards block grants was made in 1968 when the Government introduced, on the initiative of the Home Office (curiously enough), a new specific grant for its urban aid programme. This was an attempt to give special help to areas of severe social deprivation within cities and towns. Though the programme has been running at a mere £5m. or so a year, it has

---

[8] *The Future Shape of Local Government Finance*, Cmnd. 4741 (H.M.S.O., 1971), Appendix 4.

encouraged some cities to undertake several projects designed to improve the quality of life in their least privileged areas.

THE RATE-SUPPORT GRANT

Central government subventions are largely paid through the rate-support grant. This is designed to support all council services which do not receive specific grants and are not self-financing. In 1969–70 it ran at almost £1,500m. By 1973–4 it had reached nearly £3,000m. a rate of increase reflecting (apart from the changed value of money) both the continued expansion of services and a steady increase in the proportion of council expenditure met from grants.[9]

The distribution of the rate-support grant between authorities is based on a complicated formula. The grant is made up of three elements: domestic, needs, and resources. The *domestic* element is a straight subsidy for the domestic ratepayer and in 1974–5 was the equivalent of a rate of ten pence in the pound. The consequence was that when a council had decided what rate to levy in 1974–5, it deducted ten pence from the total before making demands on domestic ratepayers.

The *needs* element of the grant is rather more complicated. Each eligible local authority (the element is paid to the major spending authorities—the counties, metropolitan districts, and London boroughs) is credited with a basic amount of so many pounds per head of population and per child of school age. But since some areas clearly experience greater demands on their resources than others, this basic amount is varied according to eight 'weighting' factors. In other words, the crude population figures are increased in varying proportions because two areas with identical population figures may have quite different needs, due to differences in the circumstances of their inhabitants, of their geography, or of both. No authority qualifies for all eight: some apply to those with a high density of population, some to those sparsely populated rural areas with a large road mileage but few rate resources; others favour authorities with large numbers of old people or with a declining population.

The final part of the grant is the *resources* element, designed to bring up to the national average the rate resources, per head of population, of all authorities that would otherwise fall below it.

[9] The ratio of rates to grants declined from 49:51 in 1959–60 to 44:56 in 1969–70 and 42:58 in 1971–2.

Since richer than average authorities are not penalized, the rate resources of different councils remain unequal despite this element.

Thus great efforts are made to divide the rate-support grant fairly between all councils; indeed the detailed formula was agreed between the associations of local authorities and the Government. But in recent years criticism of the grant has grown, especially among the largest cities. Despite the weighting factors and the resources element, the grant is said to be dominated by the basic rate of payment per head of population; this penalizes areas which have major social problems and are losing population at the same time. Manchester, for example, declined in population from 655,000 in 1963 to 542,000 in 1971. Its grant as a result corresponded to a declining proportion of its expenditure at a time when for the country as a whole this proportion was rising. The problem of securing a fair distribution of the grant between areas with differing needs was recognized by the Government in its review of local government finance, published in 1971 as a Green Paper for discussion,[10] and discussions have been in progress since then with the local authority associations in an effort to improve the formula. A further consultation paper, issued in June 1973, foreshadowed legislation designed to extend the rate-support grant by absorbing several of the remaining specific grants within it and to improve the distribution formula to ensure that the varying needs of councils are more accurately reflected. These changes were enacted by the Local Government Act of 1974.[11]

Deciding the total size of the rate-support grant also causes controversy from time to time. Though in theory the Government has complete control of this decision, what happens in practice is more complicated, as the events preceding the announcement of the grant for 1973–4 well illustrate.[12]

The grant is always announced after a series of meetings, the last of which is a statutory one (laid down by Act of Parliament) between the Government and the local authority associations. In the

[10] Department of the Environment, *The Future Shape of Local Government Finance*, Cmnd. 4741 (H.M.S.O., 1971).

[11] In Greater London the resources of the boroughs are made more even by a 'rate equalization scheme' as well as through the distribution of the rate-support grant. Under the scheme the richer London boroughs contribute to a pool from which the poorer ones benefit. The 1972 act makes provision for such schemes to operate in the six metropolitan counties, but only if all the districts agree (an unlikely event).

[12] For details see *Municipal Review*, February 1973, Supplement, pp. 31–2.

summer and autumn of 1972 these meetings took place against a background of economic difficulties which led the government to adopt a counter-inflation policy restricting pay and price rises. Rates being a price which people have to pay, the Government was anxious to avoid major rate rises in April 1973. In any case a revaluation of all property was due to take effect from that date and this would affect many domestic ratepayers adversely.

The government recognized that local authority expenditure must continue to expand even if the standard of services was to be only marginally improved, and during the earlier stage of negotiations it made various concessions in reply to local authority forecasts of large potential rate increases in 1973. The crucial question was then what proportion of relevant local expenditure should be met by grant. The Government proposed 59½ per cent, a higher figure than in any previous year, the associations 60½ per cent, and agreement was eventually reached on 60 per cent. The views of the two sides about the total of expenditure on which this proportion was to be based also diverged, by £52m., even after a series of mutual compromises. But at the concluding statutory meeting a final government concession of £15m. was made, and agreement on the level (fixed at sixpence) of the domestic element was also reached.

These negotiations demonstrate that, however strong the Government's position may seem, its relations with local government, even over questions of grant, are far from dictatorial. Central government must win the co-operation of councils if the procedure is to work smoothly. Negotiations therefore could not be limited to the statutory meeting. Councils retain the right to levy whatever rate they wish, and if they think their income from grants inadequate they can increase the rate-demand—and tell the local electorate to blame the Government. In the end, however, central government takes the decision on grants and can overrule local objections, and in the background there is always the threat of tighter central control. But for all these reasons both central and local government make strenuous efforts to resolve financial differences.

THE RATING SYSTEM

English local authorities still have but one source of tax income: the rate, levied on the occupier of fixed property (whether domestic, commercial, or industrial) by reference to two figures: (a) the rateable value of the property (say £100), multiplied by (b) the number of pence in the pound (say 50) determined afresh by the council annually, resulting in a rate demand of 5,000 pence or £50. Unfortunately for local government, the rate is an unpopular and in many ways unsatisfactory tax. First, the amount levied is only very roughly based on ability to pay. Every property is given a value by the district valuer (a national civil servant of the inland revenue department), based on the annual rent which its owner might theoretically obtain from it. Broadly speaking, there is some reasonable correlation between rateable values and incomes, in so far as richer people occupy the more valuable houses. Such general correlation, however, cannot persuade a citizen that the rating system is fair if he is a widower living on a small pension when his neighbour, occupying a similar house but with two or three wage-earning 'children' still at home, pays the same sum in annual rates.

Secondly, even though better houses occupied by the comparatively wealthy are given a rateable value higher than poorer property, the differential between good and less good property is much smaller than that between the incomes of, say, the executive and the working man. The Allen Committee in 1965 found that where the disposable income of a household was £312 per annum, rate payments accounted for 8·2 per cent of it. In households with an income in excess of £1,560 the proportion was 2·2 per cent.[13] Rates are, therefore, a regressive tax: the richer you are, the smaller proportion of your income is taken from you in rates. Since the publication of the Allen Report a series of increasingly generous rebate schemes have been introduced to mitigate the impact of rates on poorer households. These may have got rid of the worst cases, but the regressive nature of the tax remains. In the early 1970s only a small minority of ratepayers (about 18 per cent) obtained a rate rebate.

Thirdly, the income which a local authority can get from rates has little inherent buoyancy. Property is revalued only every ten years or so: in theory every five years, but actual post-war revaluations have been in 1956, 1963, and 1973. And this has two effects. On the one hand a council which needs to increase its expenditure on services has constantly to increase the number of pence per pound of rateable value which it demands. This cannot be welcome to the ratepayer, especially since the total sum demanded, though it can be paid in monthly instalments, covers a whole year. On the other hand, when a revaluation at last takes place the new value of some

[13] *Report of the Committee of Inquiry into the Impact of Rates on Households*, Cmnd. 2582 (H.M.S.O., 1965), Ch. 10.

properties reflects an increase higher than the average, so that some occupiers receive a rate bill even larger than they feared. This may in fact be fair enough, for the relative attraction of different types of property varies from one time to another, but it increases yet further the unpopularity of rates.

Because of these and other[14] criticisms of the rating system, efforts have constantly been made to find alternative or additional local taxes. Petrol, sales, income, and pay-roll taxes have been discussed, and each in turn has been rejected by the Government. Rates raised more than £1,800m. in 1971–2. They are easy to administer, compared with any of the alternatives (collection costs amount only to a little over 1 per cent). Nor is any government likely to allow one of its own buoyant taxes to be transferred to local government. Probably the best that can be expected in the foreseeable future is a more regular revaluation and still more sophisticated systems of rebates, designed to lessen the regressive character of rates.

Meanwhile, despite all its defects the rating system is indispensable to local government. It is the one independent source of income of any significance. Because of public hostility to the system, it may not in practice be politically feasible for a council to raise its rate more than the minimum needed to maintain and marginally improve its services. But a council is in a position to pioneer a new service without the need for central government approval or financial aid. This marginal flexibility is crucial, for developments which improve the local quality of life need not always be expensive. Further, if rates were replaced or supplemented by more complex and less predictable local taxes, Parliament might think it necessary to make a local council's budget subject to central government approval, as it already is in France and many other countries. In England no such approval has ever been required. This freedom is a crucial element in the tradition of English local government, and though in theory there is no reason why it should not survive the abolition of rates, there would be at least a risk of losing it if ever the present local taxation system were revolutionized. Certainly the need for

[14] In 1929 occupiers of agricultural land and buildings were excused from all liability for rates, as a means of subsidizing farmers at a time of agricultural depression, and no government has dared to correct the anomaly. The maximum rating of 50 per cent on continuously empty property was often viewed as being insufficient to persuade owners to find tenants, and the 1974 Local Government Act doubled this.

central approval of a council's budget would mark a grave diminishing of freedom. It would undoubtedly deter many able elected members from serving on a council and might mean the loss to local government of some of its best financial staff. As it is, the central government can only exhort local authorities to expand or curtail their financial activities in terms such as those used in a White Paper at the time of the economic crisis of 1968:

The government expects that in 1969–70 local authorities as a whole will restrain the level of their expenditure so that it does not in total exceed a figure in the region of 3 per cent in real terms above what has already been agreed for purposes of the exchequer contribution in 1968–69.[15]

No doubt most councils responded sympathetically, yet not all could achieve the Government's target. Nor could they in 1973 when the Government's counter-inflation policy restrained prices and incomes by law. Despite the highest rate-support grant ever agreed (following the negotiations discussed earlier), the Government's request to councils for only minimum rate rises in 1973–4 did not prevent large increases in many areas.

AUDIT CONTROL

At some essential points, then, the finances of a council are free from central government control. Approval of the annual budget is not necessary nor is its form prescribed. The council is free to fix its rate in the pound each year. Charges for services, where permissible, are usually for the council to determine. There are regulations about the keeping of accounts, but these lay down only general principles and leave the council free to fashion its own style of financial management.

But there are some restrictions. In particular an authority cannot budget for a deficiency or surplus, though it can include in estimates a reasonable sum for working balances and contingencies. It can build up reserves only within the limits laid down by Parliament. The great bulk of expenditure can be only on services specifically allowed by law. Some Acts of Parliament give ministers power to approve charges: for example library fines. The police and other specific grants are paid only on approved expenditure. Capital expenditure is, as we have seen, closely controlled.

And in addition to these restrictions there is audit control. The

[15] *Public Expenditure in 1968–9 and 1969–70*, Cmnd. 3515 (H.M.S.O., 1968).

accounts of councils must be audited each year by an approved auditor, either the district auditor (a national civil servant appointed by the Department of the Environment)[16] or a private one chosen from a list approved by the Secretary of State. The audit is public and interested citizens may inspect the books, question the auditor about the accounts, and object to them.

Over the years control by audit has been highly controversial. Most people accept the need for external audit to prevent fraud and corruption. Most feel that it is helpful for local treasurers to have this regular contact with auditors who can pass on to them valuable new accountancy ideas. Controversy begins over the power of the district auditor to surcharge councillors and officers for illegal expenditure, financial losses through misconduct, or failure to bring items of expenditure into the accounts.[17]

A major difficulty has been the definition of 'illegal'. This has in the past been taken to include expenditure which the auditor considers to be unreasonable on the grounds that if a local authority spends excessively on a service this is contrary to Parliament's intentions. Well-known post-war examples have concerned the rents of council housing in areas where the authority has heavily subsidized them from the general rate fund. In 1960, for example, several St. Pancras borough councillors were surcharged: they had to repay the amount in question and, where the sum exceeded £500 (increased to £2,000 in 1974), they were excluded from serving as a councillor for five years.

Despite the recommendation of the Maud Committee that the surcharge should be abolished, the district auditor retains this power under the Local Government Act of 1972, though its provisions make it quite clear that he is concerned with expenditure which is contrary to law rather than with unreasonableness. But the act gives all authorities the right to choose between the district auditor and an approved private auditor (previously only boroughs had this choice, and then only for some of their accounts). The latter does not have the right to surcharge, but must report the facts to the Secretary of State, who may order the district auditor to undertake an extraordinary audit of the particular account in

[16] There are well over 500 audit and supporting staff organized on a regional basis under the Chief Inspector of Audit.

[17] In the last two cases the auditor himself issues the surcharge. In the case of illegal expenditure he has to apply (since the 1972 act) to the High Court for a declaration of illegality.

question. Should he concur with the private auditor, he may then issue the surcharge or go to the courts.

It is perhaps a measure of the improved image of the district auditor in recent years that there has so far been little sign of a mass move by local authorities in favour of private audit. Since the St. Pancras case there have been few major clashes between local government and the district auditor.[18] In fact there has been a significant decline in surcharging by district auditors since the 1920s and 1930s and the few cases each year usually relate to minor matters. But the advisory functions of district auditors have become increasingly important. The controversy about their legal powers may continue but it has lost much of the heat generated in the mid-1920s when after the famous Poplar case George Lansbury, the prominent Labour Party politician, and his fellow councillors were sent to prison.[19]

Although there are many controversial aspects of local government finance, the most important is the rating system. Successive generations of national and local politicians have condemned it as unsatisfactory and unfair; one recent Minister of Housing and Local Government (Mr. Richard Crossman) announced in 1965 that he intended to replace it 'with a new local tax, fair, intelligible and capable of being administered reasonably efficiently'. Yet the system continues to operate much as it used to do, with only the addition of rebates and the domestic element of the rate-support grant as sops to the critic.

Mr. Crossman's strong words were not followed by firm action. The Royal Institute of Public Administration (RIPA) shortly afterwards produced a lengthy report for the Redcliffe-Maud Commission favouring the transfer of vehicle-based taxes (notably the fuel tax) to local government but also suggesting that a local income tax was feasible. Study groups of the Institute of Municipal Treasurers and Accountants (I.M.T.A.) broadly concurred with the RIPA's view, and the Redcliffe-Maud Commission added its support, though without favouring any particular tax. The Com-

---

[18] The best-known was the case of Clay Cross Urban District Council in 1973. The council declined to raise the rents of its houses in accordance with the 1972 Housing Finance Act: its dispute with the auditor was not primarily about reasonableness. See *Asher* v. *Lacey* [1973] 3 All E.R. 1008.

[19] For the story of this *cause célèbre* see B. Keith-Lucas, 'Poplarism', *Public Law*, Spring 1962, 52—80.

mission did not envisage the abolition of the rating system which was too productive to be done away with. Instead the Commission strongly recommended that the system should be supplemented by a second and more buoyant local tax.[20]

The prospect at that time of a more rational set of local government boundaries also seemed a good omen for reform, for an argument used against some alternative taxes was that they could not be administered sensibly or fairly while boundaries were archaic. For example, so many people crossed boundaries to their place of work that there would be endless questions whether local income tax should be payable where a person lived or where he worked. 'Petrol tax wars' could also be envisaged if a council kept the petrol-tax rate low to attract motorists away from its neighbours. By the end of the 1960s a radical reform of local government finance seemed to be possible.

The Government's review of local government finance turned out in the end to be all the more disappointing for these expectations. Its 1971 Green Paper[21] held out no hope of major reform in the foreseeable future. The alternative local taxes which had been strongly canvassed in the late 1960s were criticized as ineffective or inoperable at reasonable cost; those who had foreseen that no government would give up a major buoyant tax were proved true prophets. It remained for the Government's consultation paper of 1973 and legislation of 1973–4 to confirm the worst fears of the pessimist. Local government continues to depend on rates and grants.

[20] Cmnd. 4040, para. 539.   [21] Cmnd. 4741.

9

Relations Between Central and Local Government

CENTRAL government plays a crucial part in English local government and, before the complex working relationships involved in that partnership can be understood, some of its main characteristics must be mentioned.

First there is the sovereignty of Parliament: all the powers and duties of all local councils are derived from Parliament and can at any time be varied by Parliament. Unlike states in a federal system, therefore, English local councils are in one sense the creatures of the nation state. Yet at the same time they are also creatures of the local community. Their essence is found in the fact that they are elected and therefore responsible to local people for the use of the taxing and other powers given them by Parliament. Here is the mark that distinguishes them fundamentally from local agents of central administration, such as the post office or the department of employment.

But, secondly, even in discharging their responsibility to local people, they cannot be allowed to use their discretion without regard for national and other interests wider than the purely local one. Parliament has therefore given certain ministers and central departments various powers and duties which involve them in local government as national partners of the local authorities.

There are several reasons for this. One is economic: in 1971 local government accounted for nearly one-third of all public expenditure. As all governments nowadays accept responsibility for the general health of the economy, no government can allow such a proportion to be free of all central control or influence. Further, control over local capital expenditure provides a comparatively easy way for the central government to alter the pattern of investment at reasonably short notice: in December 1973 a reduction in public capital expenditure of some £1200m. over the period to March 1975 was announced and much of this sum had to come from local services; in 1971, when unemployment was at a dangerously high level, local government was encouraged to step up certain kinds of expenditure. Nor can a government be expected to provide local authorities with large grants-in-aid without having some control over their destiny. Again, services provided by local councils, such as education, housing, and transport, are often the subject of national political debate.

These issues are therefore important to the national political parties, and ministers cannot escape a large responsibility for them. Public opinion demands that services should be provided fairly for all citizens irrespective of the locality in which they happen to live. Moreover the mass media operate primarily on a national rather than a local level and can quickly make any local failings clear to a national audience. The role of central government is therefore to ensure that at least minimum standards of statutory services are everywhere achieved.

A third characteristic of the English system distinguishes it from overseas practice such as that of France. The national interest in local government is not protected by any one central department of state with general responsibility for control or supervision of local councils, such as that of the French Department of the Interior, nor is there any such officer in England as the French prefect. True, the Secretary of State for the Environment and his department is specially concerned with local government as is no other cabinet member or other part of Whitehall; one of his team of junior ministers is called Minister for Local Government and Development, another is Minister for Transport Industries, another for Housing and Construction. But the Secretary of State has no general power of intervention beyond those given him by particular statutes, and there are other members of the cabinet who have similar specific powers and duties for major parts of local government: in particular for education, social services, police (the Home Secretary), and consumer affairs. All these ministers and their departments are therefore part and parcel of local government and it is the continuous collaboration between them and local councils that is the main subject of this chapter. Moreover the style of that partnership varies subtly from one department to another, partly because of differences in the statutes that concern each of them, partly from their various historical traditions, and partly for personal reasons: the attitude of individual ministers and, still more important, the differing degrees of formality with which central and local officers behave towards each other.

Fourthly, besides this heterogeneous nature of the relationship between central departments and the local council, there is a great variety in the directions, controls, and interventions whereby the national and local partners work together. At one extreme there is the order or regulation, made with the authority of parliamentary statute by a department, which when approved has the force of law and is properly described as delegated legislation. At the other, there is the consultation paper, put out by a department for discussion and carrying no sanction save the force of argument. Between the two extremes there are circulars, draft schemes, guide lines, approvals, and many different kinds of correspondence. But however much these forms of central action differ, whether in tone or purpose, the characteristic practice of departments is to *consult*: if at all possible, to reach agreement; if necessary, to compromise; at the least, to avoid public confrontation.

This consultation begins before ministers either exercise discretionary powers or ask Parliament to pass new legislation. Departments have close relations with the major associations of authorities and with other bodies representing particular interests in local government (the institute of municipal treasurers and accountants, the association of public health inspectors, the institute of housing managers, and dozens of others). Such bodies provide valuable sounding boards and can consider new ideas in terms of practical applicability. They also frequently initiate proposals based on their collective experience of administration. Two-way consultation between the Government and these bodies is accepted as a regular convention, and local government is quick to complain when it considers that ministers have failed to observe it. This occurred in July 1970, for example, when the secretary of state for education and science published a circular giving councils greater freedom over their pattern of secondary education. Though the contents of the circular came as no surprise and were broadly welcomed in local government circles, complaint of a lack of prior consultation was still made. The word, therefore, which best sums up the mutual relationship of central and local government is partnership.

CONTROL AND DIRECTION

Broad general controls are to be found in almost all Acts of Parliament that concern local government. But few acts go into detail about the method of provision of local services and much discretion is left both to the individual councils and to ministers.

The degree of control and supervision varies widely as between functions. To some extent it is determined by the wording of the appropriate act. In some services the relevant minister is to provide 'general guidance' (Local Authority Social Services Act, 1970); in others the minister's responsibility is far more positive. Section one of the 1944 Education Act lays down that the minister has a 'duty . . . to secure the effective execution by local authorities, under his control and direction, of the national policy for providing a varied and comprehensive educational service in every area'. The Public Libraries and Museums Act 1964 also uses the term 'duty', this time to 'superintend, and promote the improvement of, the public library services provided by local authorities . . . and to secure the proper discharge by local authorities of the functions in relation to libraries conferred on them as library authorities by or under this Act'.

In practice such broad statements leave ministers wide discretion. What, for example, constitutes 'the proper discharge' of library functions? What does the 'effective execution' of educational services mean when a specific case is considered? Ministers and their departments are free to interpret such phrases in their own way, though they may be called on to defend their interpretation at any time in Parliament and sometimes in a court of law. These statements of principle, however, give an indication of the likely degree of government involvement in local activities. The Department of Health and Social Security, for example, is likely to have a less intimate relationship with local councils than is the Department of Education and Science.

In practice, more important than powers of general control are the provisions of acts about specific points at which ministers may or must exercise their discretion in elaborating the intentions of Parliament. These powers are frequently exercised in the form of delegated legislation, supplementing the parliamentary act with regulations of a more detailed kind which are normally approved by Parliament without debate. One example, of the hundreds dealing with local government that could be cited, concerns the 'boarding out' of children committed to the care of a local authority. This indicates the way in which more detailed controls than those included in an act are exercised by government departments.[1]

The Children Act of 1948 places local authorities under a general duty to board out children in their care wherever this is practicable and desirable. The act does not lay down any detailed arrangements to be followed by a council in supervising such children but gives the minister (then the Home Secretary, now the Secretary of State for Health and Social Security) the power to issue regulations binding on all councils. These regulations had to be presented to Parliament in the form of a statutory instrument which did not require debate.

The relevant instrument (No. 1377 of 1955) controls boarding-out arrangements in great detail. Before a child goes to a foster home a social worker has to prepare a detailed report on the home: its physical condition and the health and character of the potential foster parents. A medical examination of the child is needed, as are regular subsequent medical inspections and visits from a social worker (even their regularity is laid down: for example, a social worker must visit the child within one month of its arrival at the home, and then within a number of weeks, between six and twelve, depending on the age of the child). Regular reviews of the child must also be undertaken, by someone who is not the social worker responsible for the case.

The object of more detailed controls is to lay down minimum standards for all children's authorities and all areas. Beyond these there is local discretion. There is nothing to prevent more frequent visits, medical inspections, and reviews than the minimum. Nor do the regulations restrict the amount paid to foster parents or control the number or proportion of children in care who may be boarded out. But they may go into great detail: at one time a council had to get specific approval of alternative arrangements from the Home Secretary if it did not board out a child committed to its care by the courts within three months of the court order being made.

SANCTIONS

There are various ways in which central departments can enforce controls. In theory they can take a council to court for failing to

[1] The example is adapted from J. A. G. Griffith, *Central Departments and Local Authorities* (Allen & Unwin, 1966), pp. 392–6.

carry out its duties, but in practice such a move is unlikely because it would have serious political consequences which no minister would normally face. Another sanction is the withdrawal of government grant, for ministers have power to reduce the amount of grant if they are not satisfied with the performance of a council. But here again there might be wide political reactions. Further, it is almost always difficult to measure the quality of a council's performance: quantity can be measured (the number of visits by social workers or of school meals consumed) but quality cannot (the visits may be short, the meals inadequate). A minister would find it hard to prove that a council was performing badly enough to justify reduction of grant unless it was failing to provide a service of any kind.

Some Acts of Parliament prescribe default powers for use when a statutory service is not provided. For example, under the Housing Finance Act of 1972 the Minister was given the power to appoint housing commissioners to calculate and collect rents in areas where a local council was not implementing the act. These powers were used in the case of Clay Cross, but default powers found in earlier housing, welfare, water, and sewage legislation seem hardly to have been used at all. Indeed, until the appointment of a housing commissioner under the 1972 act, the refusal of Coventry and St. Pancras to provide for civil defence were almost the only known cases in which default powers were used.

Inspection and audit give central government other means of enforcing its controls. Inspection is restricted to four services: education, police, fire, and the social services. In the first and last cases, the main role of inspectors is advisory, though they report any glaring failures to fulfil minimum standards, such as those concerned with boarding-out. The inspectors of fire and police combine the roles of adviser and inspector, and adverse reports on brigades and forces are not unknown.

The audit of accounts has already been discussed. For the positive enforcement of controls it is unlikely to be important. Should a council spend more than a prescribed maximum the auditor would declare the expenditure illegal, but few acts or orders lay down financial maxima. One example is the 1972 Local Government Act, which permits expenditure, in the interests of the area, of up to a two-penny rate on any service which cannot be provided under other legislation.

No authority is likely to refrain in practice from undertaking a major obligation unless that duty has been placed on it in an atmosphere of political strife. In such legislation, and the Housing Finance Act of 1972 was an example, the government of the day is bound to ensure that it has adequate powers of enforcement. But normally the content of a control reflects agreement between local and central government and emerges from lengthy consultation. A council is then unlikely to flaunt the law deliberately for it cannot expect to have public or local government opinion on its side. Of course some detailed controls may be disobeyed for unavoidable reasons: a shortage of social workers, for example, could cause failures to undertake statutory visits under the boarding-out regulations.

INTERVENTION

By intervention is meant the use of particular controls which differ from general control and direction in two ways. First, they are exercised by government departments over an individual council rather than local authorities in general. Secondly, they are interventions by a minister or department in order to decide whether or not a council may do something that it intends to do: administrative initiative lies locally rather than at the centre. Such controls take up far more of the time of central civil servants than do general ones, because they involve the minister in individual cases coming forward from hundreds of different councils.

There are three main types of intervention. First, there are local schemes for the future running of services which have to be submitted for approval to the minister. Secondly, there are rationing controls, where the minister is deciding on the precise way in which national resources should be allocated between areas. Finally, there are controls over the appointment of certain officers. Like all classifications, this one leaves some issues on the borderline, as the following discussion of each category will illustrate.

Approval of schemes has become a common method of central control since the second world war. Between 1944 and 1950 Acts of Parliament required the new authorities for education, welfare and health to submit local development schemes for the approval of the appropriate minister. Development plans showing future patterns of land-use were also required under town planning legislation. All these have by now become historical documents, but more recently, in 1965, education authorities were asked to produce plans for secondary-school reorganization which would accord with the wish of the government of the day to have comprehensive education in all areas. Without a change in the Education Act of 1944 the production of such schemes was not obligatory, and some authorities declined to comply with the Government's request. Structure plans have now replaced the old development plans in the town planning field, following legislation in 1968, and more recently still, in 1972, councils responsible for social services were instructed to produce ten-year development schemes.

Scheme approval contains elements of both general and particular control. The general element lies in the obligation to produce a scheme and sometimes in the content of the scheme (structure plans have to follow a set format; education schemes under the 1944 act had to comply with a statutory list of contents). The particular element lies in the detailed proposals coming from each authority. These may be affected by exhortations and advice from government departments (the recent ten-year plans for social services were requested by the Secretary of State in a circular outlining certain targets at which authorities might care to aim), but they reflect the desires of the local council to develop its services in the way which it feels is most appropriate for its area.

Secondly, the short-term aims of a council, whenever they involve capital expenditure, are subject to rationing controls. The operation of loan sanction, which has already been discussed, means that the bulk of capital expenditure continues to be on key-sector projects— schools, houses, roads, homes, workshops, day centres, and so on— each individual project requiring approval.

Though each central department has its own methods for approval of capital projects, in all such work they are reacting to local pro-posals—modifying, approving, or forbidding them. There may be general controls over certain aspects of the proposals: a local education authority, for example, must ensure that its detailed plans for a new school comply with regulations about building standards laid down in delegated legislation. The authority will also be aware from ministerial policy statements what type of project is most likely to be approved. For example, at the end of 1972 the Secretary of State for Education and Science announced that she proposed to allow local authorities to spend £30m. on the expansion of nursery education. In February 1973 she asked each authority to submit proposals for expenditure in this field. Her request was incorporated in a circular which outlined the sort of project to which she would be most favourably disposed, such as nursery classes attached to primary schools.

The third type of intervention concerns staffing. In the police service this is taken to extreme lengths with the approval by the Home Secretary of detailed establishment figures and recruitment policy for each separate force. Other examples relate to the appointments of chief constables and fire officers, and of directors of social services. These involve two government departments (both police and fire are the responsibility of the Home Office), each with its own methods of operation. In general, however, the pattern involves the submission of a short list of candidates to the relevant ministry by the council, and the approval or amendment of this list before the council interviews and makes its choice. Until 1973 the same procedure applied to appointments of directors of education.

An interesting instance of this control in action occurred in 1970 when the Local Authority Social Services Act was passed. County, county borough, and London borough councils proceeded to advertise the new posts of director of social services. Children's and welfare officers naturally hoped to be appointed as their separate departments were to disappear, but they were not the only candidates.[2] Some councils were anxious to appoint officers with proven managerial rather than professional ability, even if they had not worked in local government previously. In December 1970 the Secretary of State revealed that, of 142 authorities who had consulted him about their short-lists, seventy-two had been told that their lists contained one or more names who could not be approved. The lists contained 404 names in all, and sixty-eight of these were not considered suitable as potential directors by the ministry.[3]

APPEALS

A further set of cases where a minister reacts to local initiative covers appeals. Here the minister acts as judge in a dispute either between a council and its citizens or between two local authorities. There are many instances where Parliament has said that ministers rather than courts of law should decide disputes and that decisions should be administrative rather than judicial. Sometimes these are referred to as quasi-judicial controls.

Appeals from individuals against a decision of a council lie mainly within the fields of planning and housing. The planning appeal (of

[2] Some medical officers, probation workers, and directors of social services in Scotland were applicants.

[3] *Hansard* (Commons), Vol. 808, Written Answers, Col. 291 (15 Dec. 1970).

which there were more than 14,000 in 1972) is a typical example. If a council refuses to give planning permission (say, for a new building or for a change in the use of an existing one) this refusal may be contested by the applicant at a public inquiry before an inspector[4] from the Department of the Environment (the parties to the dispute may sometimes agree to a postal inquiry through the submission of written representations). On small matters the inspector will himself make the decision; on larger issues his report and recommendations will be passed through the ministry and, in very important cases, may even come to the minister himself for decision. The inspector's recommendations are sometimes, but not often, overruled by a minister, and the report of the inspector is nowadays always published (this means that a citizen is entitled to have access to it, not that it can be bought at a bookshop).

Another example is the compulsory purchase order (C.P.O.), made on property or land. Normally some 500 are issued each year by local authorities. A council may make one of these for various reasons: because it wishes to build a road across the area, a school, a senior citizens' home, or some other project. The property it is seeking to obtain may be classified as unfit or as fit; if unfit (for human habitation) the owner can object to the classification; if fit, he can argue that the need for the purchase has not been proved. Whether there is a dispute or not, the order needs approval by the ministry. A dispute, once again, involves a local inquiry before a departmental inspector.

Nor are planning and housing the only fields within which central departments exercise appellate functions. Another is education. Here legislation includes a section commonly known as parental choice. Councils are expected to take into account the wishes of parents when deciding on the future education of a child, and appeals are sometimes made to the Department of Education and Science. Recently one parent in a northern town appealed to the minister because the council, having decided to apply a school-zoning scheme more strictly, sought to send his younger child to a different school from that attended by his elder one. After an investigation of the facts, the minister upheld the parent's view that the younger child should go to the same school as the elder.

Disputes between council and council which cannot be resolved

---

[4] Although the title 'inspector' also applies to the education, fire, police, and social services, the function of the planning inspectorate is quite different from the other four whose relations with local councils are less formal and more regular.

locally are, fortunately, not common. But they are not unknown, particularly in the planning and housing fields. During the 1950s and 1960s most of the major cities and conurbations were 'exporting' population to surrounding suburban and rural areas, and this led to conflict on occasion. This was particularly the case in the north-west where Manchester was in dispute with councils in Cheshire. On several occasions the minister was forced to mediate: in the 1950s he refused Manchester permission to build overspill estates in the villages of Lymm and Mobberley; a decade later he agreed to the city obtaining large sites by compulsory purchase in Wilmslow.[5]

These two decades also saw constant boundary disputes in many parts of England, particularly during the reviews of the 1958 local government commission. Again the minister had to exercise an appellate function when proposals of the commission were contested locally. That commission's work, and that of the 1972 Local Government Boundary Commission, were discussed in Chapters 3 and 4. Hoping to avoid the arcrimony of future boundary disputes, the Government announced in 1972 that it planned to establish a convention that the new boundary commission's proposals would normally be accepted and implemented in full.

CONSULTATION

The relations between central and local government discussed above are worked out in a variety of ways. In particular cases interaction may be for a brief period only, but over most of the field there is constant and almost continuous contact between local councils and the centre. The work of the education and other inspectorates is an example. Another is the activity of the local authority associations, representing the collective interests of the councils. Whether the initiative for change in the general organization or particular powers of local government comes from the centre or from councils, there is a continuing two-way partnership.

Such consultation is for a variety of purposes. Often they cannot be distinguished clearly one from another but they may be broadly classified as follows: mutual information; research and the pooling of experience; mutual persuasion and negotiation.

The collection and dissemination of information is a subject that naturally brings central and local government together. Much

[5] For the story of this dispute see J. M. Lee and B. Wood, *The Scope of Local Initiative* (Martin Robertson, 1974), Ch. 2.

information about individual areas is collected and published on a national basis, either by the national organizations of authorities or by central government. The institute of municipal treasurers and accountants (I.M.T.A.), for example, has long published unit-cost statistics of the major local government services. Each year a questionnaire goes out from the institute to each local authority requesting these statistics and outlining a method of calculation designed to obtain comparable data. The great majority of authorities co-operate.

During the last twenty years local government has itself built up four national bodies each of which contributes to a central store of information and knowledge that both local and central government can use. The Local Government Training Board (L.G.T.B.), which has already been discussed, compiled the first comprehensive national survey of local government staff in 1972–3, and gave invaluable advice to councils about training needs arising from the 1972 act. It produced a 'training for change' package designed for use within an authority, and promoted additional courses. The Local Government Information Office (L.G.I.O.), as its name implies, provides a common service for all councils and a centre of information that any of the communication media can consult. It makes available posters and other material relating to all kinds of subject, such as home safety and local elections. In 1973 it distributed more than a million leaflets explaining the new local government structure. The Local Government Operational Research Unit (L.G.O.R.U.) has undertaken a large number of research projects for individual authorities. Some of its best known early work was in the field of refuse disposal where its studies helped significantly to rationalize the service. Finally, the Local Authorities Management Services and Computers Committee (LAMSAC) has played a major part in developing computers and other management aids. About half its net cost is met by grant from the department of the environment.

In the period before these recent local government developments it was central departments that did most to disseminate information, and they still do much. Ambulance, refuse disposal, and development control (i.e. planning application) statistics have been collected and made available for many years and these enable the performance of individual councils to be compared. The comprehensive *Statistics of Education* published by the department of education and science give data broken down by region, while the environment department's *Local Government Financial Statistics* give detailed national figures of expenditure and income. Other publications include technical information such as the planning and design bulletins of the department of the environment. Information is also disseminated on a regular personal basis through the four central government inspectorates mentioned above and through the district auditor (for example, about good accounting practices). Finally, the specialist local government press (*Local Government Chronicle, Municipal Journal*, etc.) and the journals of the professional bodies, are important channels of communication.

This exchange of information and pooling of experience is of great importance to both central and local government. It enables central departments to obtain a greater understanding of the activities of particular councils and stimulates new national policy initiatives. Councils on their side have much to learn from experiments undertaken in other areas, and the interchange of information about them leads to constant improvement in techniques and standards of service. Information flows thus encourage healthy competition between councils as they vie with each other for reputation.

Research is a second subject in which councils and departments interact, again in an attempt to improve standards. Sometimes central government itself initiates or sponsors research, as when the Department of Education and Science joined with the Social Science Research Council in asking Dr. A. H. Halsey of Oxford University to lead and co-ordinate a series of studies into educational priority areas, the results of which were published in 1972. On other occasions it promotes research jointly with either individual councils or the local government associations. For example, in 1973 the Department of the Environment agreed to sponsor a study of participation in planning by paying half the salaries of several officers employed locally by councils to help the public formulate its views and communicate with the planners. The department has also set up planning research teams at a regional level jointly with the local planning authorities in the area. The first produced the *South East Strategy* in 1970 and others cover the north and north-west regions. Finally, councils themselves are undertaking much research, particularly in the social services. Some have copied the G.L.C. in setting up a central research unit, often under the direct control of the chief executive.

But information and research are of limited value unless action follows, either locally or centrally. Sometimes this leads departments to ask Parliament for additional powers either for themselves or for local authorities. Sometimes existing legislation is sufficient when applied in a new way. In either case action involves central and local government in mutual persuasion and negotiation.

Usually persuasion takes the gentlemanly form of written representation, departmental circular, ministerial speech, or private meeting. But occasionally more dramatic methods are used, as in some areas following the passage of the Housing Finance Act of 1972 when certain councils publicly declared their refusal to increase council house rents. Nor was this an isolated example: a few years earlier some councils took a similar line over the reduction in free school milk and some over the question of comprehensive schools.

These instances of conflict normally arise only over party political issues when a local council is controlled by a different party from that of the Government in Westminster. Far more common are issues that raise mainly administrative or technical questions which can be discussed amicably at private meetings. Purely local issues (for example, when a council protests against the low number of projects approved out of its submitted programme) can also be resolved privately: indeed this is in the interest of both sides, for the department has no wish to be flooded with local deputations and the council is aware that if its own protest is known to have prevailed many other authorities will seek additional concessions.

It is because each side needs the co-operation of the other at key points that persuasion and negotiation often succeed. Despite its statutory powers the Government cannot do without local authorities, to implement national policies and collaborate as partners in adapting national objectives to local circumstance. Despite its size, England is extremely diverse in character. National policies must consist of general statements which can be interpreted in more than one way when it comes to specific implementation. At the same time local government cannot afford to lose the respect of ministers, M.P.s, and the national political parties: if it did it would have no future. It stands only to lose from persistent conflict with the central government.

Two examples illustrate the central–local relationship in action. The first is the attempt by the Labour Government of 1964–70 to further its general policy of favouring comprehensive secondary schools instead of the traditional selection of pupils for grammar, technical, and modern schools. Despite the strong wording of section one of the 1944 Education Act, discussed earlier, it was by no means certain that local authorities could be made to adopt a comprehensive system. Twice the Government tried persuasion. First, in 1965 it 'requested' local authorities to propose comprehensive schemes. Secondly, in 1966 it stated that no *new* secondary schools could be built unless they were designed as comprehensives. Several authorities still failed to submit a scheme acceptable to the Minister, and here persuasion failed. Indeed by 1970 the Government had decided on legislation and a bill was put before Parliament to deprive councils of their discretion in this matter. Before it could become law the 1970 general election took place and, for a variety of reasons, the Government fell.

The pre-planning of the 1972 Local Government Act provides a second illustration. In February 1971 the Government published a white paper setting down the proposed general framework for a new local government structure and promising legislation in 1972–3. Many details were left open in the white paper (the question of payment of councillors, for example, and the exact division of responsibilities between counties and districts), and full consultation on the whole plan was promised.

The rest of 1971 proved to be a year of intense discussion. Individual councils gave their reactions to the proposed new boundaries, associations of authorities and other interested bodies discussed more general questions. The Government produced papers for consultation: more than twenty between February 1971 and the publication of the bill in November, and several others during and after the passage of the bill; interested bodies replied with written comments, and there were private meetings on particular issues. The bodies consulted in this process numbered no fewer than ninety-nine;[6] nor were the government papers mere discussion documents but often contained concrete suggestions. Many of these were quite acceptable to local government; others were not. For example, the proposed single structure for planning staff, designed to avoid the separation of county and district teams, was heavily criticized—and later abandoned by the Government.

Three general conclusions may be drawn from these examples. First, both central and local government are well accustomed to

---

[6] Following criticism the papers were made generally available to interested persons. But the tight timetable imposed by the white paper meant that the officers of the associations and other bodies had little time in which to consult widely with their members.

negotiate: indeed there is an unwritten convention that consultation should take place on all important and many less important
matters. Negotiations over the wording of the 1965 circular on
secondary reorganization, for example, took six months.[7] Secondly,
this convention gives the associations of local authorities and other
national bodies (e.g. societies of chief officers and professional
institutions) an important role to play as regular links with central
government and spokesmen for local government as a whole.
Finally, ministers are not anxious to increase statutory controls on
local government so long as negotiated agreement remains possible.
The 1964–70 Labour Government waited nearly five years before
deciding to legislate on comprehensive education. The Conservatives in 1971 preferred private consultation to imposed solutions
about details of the new local government structure.

   The debate in recent years about central–local relations has
largely concentrated on the question of central control, and most of
it has been critical of current practice. Proposals for change in the
relationship have come from both the Maud Committee and the
Redcliffe-Maud Commission, and range from radical suggestions
for councils to have a 'general competence', enabling them to do
anything not specifically excluded by Act of Parliament, to minor
proposals for the repeal of a host of detailed controls.
   Government response to criticism has been an acceptance that
local authorities should be given more freedom and a willingness to
review its own behaviour. Following the publication of its White
Paper on reorganization in February 1971, the Government
produced a list of 1,254 statutory controls and promised to negotiate
with the local authority associations and reduce the list to bare
essentials. The 1972 Local Government Act repealed some controls
(over the appointment of certain officers and committees, for
example) and legislation reduced the list still further in 1974.
   Despite these moves the feeling remains that little significant
relaxation is in prospect. Government statements profess a general
willingness to reconsider central controls but specific action by
individual ministers seems to run counter to this principle. Since the
start of discussions about the 'list of 1,254', for instance, new legislation has prevented education authorities from providing free milk to
the older children at primary schools and has removed from local
authorities their power to fix the rents of council houses. The

7 M. Kogan, *The Politics of Education* (Penguin, 1971), p. 189.

relaxation of loan sanction in 1970 has already been discussed, but detailed project approval remains in all the major services.

Broad intent has seldom been matched by action, and the attitude of ministers to local government continues to vary with their political determination to achieve national results. Anthony Crosland, Secretary of State for Education and Science from 1965 to 1967, described the problem thus:[8]

All governments and ministers are a bit schizophrenic about their relationships with local authorities. On the one hand they genuinely believe the ringing phrases they use about how local government should have more power and freedom. On the other hand a Labour government hates it when Tory councils pursue education or housing policies of which it disapproves, and exactly the same is true of a Tory government with Labour councils.

Unless and until public opinion begins to support local government more vehemently in its claims for freedom, the situation will not change radically. Lady Sharp, a former permanent secretary at the Ministry of Housing and Local Government and a member of the Redcliffe-Maud Commission, has written:

The traditional view of the ministry is that local government ought to be allowed as much freedom of decision as possible. But in an age when public opinion demands that central government should take more and more responsibility for the adequacy of all public services, this objective seems to retreat ever further into the distance.[9]

In a country dominated by nation-wide mass media and national political parties this may be inevitable.

Whatever the prospects may be, the present relationship between central and local government is far more complex than that of master and servant or principal and agent. There is a wide range of central controls but these are normally exercised only after full discussion and genuine effort to seek agreement. Consultation and negotiation precede almost every action by the central government. The latter negotiates from strength but it has no wish for an open confrontation with local government. Only policies with an intense political content are pursued without regard for local hostility, and even here concessions may be made. The 1965 circular which asked local education authorities to produce plans for the reorganization of secondary education made stronger demands in its draft form than

[8] Kogan, op. cit., p. 171.
[9] Evelyn Sharp, *The Ministry of Housing and Local Government* (Allen & Unwin, 1969), p. 67.

when it emerged from consultation. More recently the Government allowed many housing authorities to increase their rents by less than the statutory amount. These councils argued that their rents were already close to the fair rent level and the Government, though sanctions were available, had no wish to press its argument at a time when some councils were threatening not to implement the 1972 Housing Finance Act.

10

Local Government and the Courts

As we saw in the last chapter, some of the duties which Parliament has imposed on local authorities are supervised and enforced directly by ministers of the central government. Where the minister has default powers he has no need to seek the assistance of the courts in enforcing the duty of the local authority, and no one other than the minister can go to court to have that particular duty enforced by other means. Thus, if a local authority fails in its statutory duty to provide temporary accommodation for those in urgent need, no citizen is entitled to resort either to 'self-help' or to the courts to oblige the local authority to act; for the minister has the default power, and that is the exclusive remedy.[1] We saw that in practice ministers very rarely use their default powers, and almost as rarely resort to the courts against local authorities; in fact court proceedings between central departments and local authorities are few and far between.

But the courts have an important part to play in local government. For relations between central and local authorities are only one aspect of the wider whole, and ministerial default powers, though important, relate only to selected matters. The very stuff of local government is found elsewhere: in the vast network of relations between on the one hand the local authority, its members and officers, and on the other the local authority and the citizens in its area, whose lives are affected by the exercise of its powers and the performance of its duties, and who themselves may have special powers and duties as electors, ratepayers, property-owners, and the

[1] *Southwark London Borough Council* v. *Williams* [1971] Ch. 734.

like. This network of relations is almost wholly defined by laws and in all but a few respects is actively regulated by the courts.

For these local government purposes, the most important court is the High Court, which has three divisions: the Queen's Bench Division (which often sits as a 'divisional court', that is with more than one judge), the Chancery Division, and the Family Division. Appeal from the High Court lies to the Court of Appeal and thence (or, sometimes, immediately) to the House of Lords. Of equal rank with the High Court are the new Crown Court (which replaces the old assizes and quarter sessions and deals with serious criminal matters) and the National Industrial Relations Court. Minor civil matters are the province of the county courts (which are not the responsibility of counties and whose areas of jurisdiction do not correspond with local government boundaries new or old); appeal lies to the Court of Appeal and House of Lords. Finally, there are the magistrates' courts, organized by central government on the basis of local government boundaries; they have wide criminal, civil, and miscellaneous (e.g. licensing) jurisdiction; appeal lies sometimes to the Crown Court, sometimes to the Family Division of the High Court, but, in local government matters, usually to the Queen's Bench Division of the High Court; further appeal from all such courts is to the Court of Appeal and thence to the House of Lords.

THE 'PERSONALITY' AND POWERS OF THE COUNCIL

Throughout this book we have spoken of a local authority as if it were an entity or person in its own right, the subject or bearer of rights, powers, and duties in much the same way as a minister, ratepayer, or elector who is a person of flesh and blood. In speaking in this way we are simply following the law, which considers each county or district council as an artificial person, corporation, or 'body corporate'. In essence, this means that when the members of a council authorize some action—the authorization being in accord with proper procedures and the action being one that is within the legally defined powers of the council—then whatever the councillors have thus authorized will be considered as the action, not of those councillors who voted in favour nor even of all the councillors, but of the council itself as a body corporate. Charges for expenses in respect of that action will be made by (or to) the council, not any of the councillors; payments will be made to (or out of) the council's funds; and any legal proceedings in relation to the action will be instituted by (or against) the council. Similarly, land and other property can be acquired, held, and disposed of by the local authority as such. The courts go so far as to say that the council itself has a reputation to gain or lose just as much as have its members individually and collectively; so a council can sue if it is itself defamed, and any damages awarded to it by the court will be paid into the funds of the council.[2]

In all this the special role of the courts is to decide, impartially and on legal not political principles, what are the precise limits within which actions, authorized by the members of a council and performed by the officers, servants, or agents of the council, can be counted as the actions of the council itself. For the fundamental principle governing all corporate bodies established by statute (as all local authorities now are) is that the corporation can do only what it is positively[3] authorized to do under the authority of a statute. Whatever is not thus authorized is *ultra vires* (outside the powers) of the corporate body, and is not that body's act in the eyes of the law.[4] The principle that governors must act within the powers assigned to them naturally applies as much to ministers as to local councils: if, for instance, a minister is authorized to approve the proposals of a local authority to reorganize its schools, and to grant his approval with such *modifications* as appear to the minister to be desirable, the courts will not allow him substantially to reject and *replace* the local authority's proposals with a scheme of his own.[5]

Nor is it unimportant for councillors to be aware of the legal limits of the powers of their council. Any councillor who votes for an expenditure which the court declares to be 'contrary to law' (for example, because it is for a purpose outside the powers of the council) may be ordered by the court to repay the whole or part of

---

[2] *Bognor Regis Urban District Council* v. *Campion* [1972] 2 Q.B. 169.

[3] 'Positively' does not mean 'expressly', for the courts have always recognized the principle now embodied in s.111 of the Local Government Act of 1972, that a local authority has power to do anything which is 'calculated to facilitate, or is conducive or incidental to' the discharge of any of the functions expressly conferred on the authority by statute.

[4] There is an important exception which, like the rule itself, is designed to uphold the rule of law: a local council will be liable (just as any other person would be) for the torts (civil wrongs, such as trespass or libel or negligently injuring) of its servants or agents if it has directly 'authorized' those wrongful acts or omissions, and it cannot escape its liability for torts (as it can always escape its liability for contracts) by showing that the act or omission in question was *ultra vires*.

[5] *Legg* v. *I.L.E.A.* [1972] 3 All E.R. 177.

it; and if the expenditure exceeds £2,000 the councillor who authorized it may be disqualified by the court from being a member of a
local authority for any specified period.[6] Of course court proceedings
are never initiated by the court itself: in the present instance
application to the court for a declaration of illegality or order to
repay must be made by the district auditor or, if the auditor fails to
do so, by any local government elector who had attended before the
auditor to object to the accounts of the local authority and who is
now aggrieved by the auditor's refusal to apply to the court.

But there are many other occasions and ways for local government electors, ratepayers, and other interested persons to be
involved in litigation with the local council itself, as distinct from its
members. Many of these legal proceedings will be initiated by the
local authority itself, to enforce statutory requirements against
inhabitants of the area: the local authority may be enforcing payment of rates by complaint before the local magistrates' court; or it
may be initiating criminal proceedings for enforcement of, say, the
Clean Air Act; or it may be suing in the county court or in the
High Court to recover expenses incurred in exercising its default
powers to make satisfactory provision for drainage of private premises
or to prevent such premises falling into an unhealthy condition.
There are many statutory standards which it is the responsibility
of local authorities to enforce against private persons and such enforcement may always involve the courts as the last resort.

THE CITIZEN'S REMEDIES AGAINST THE COUNCIL

Equally often, on the other hand, it will be citizens and private
concerns that will be seeking the aid of the courts in a dispute with
the local authority. And usually the dispute will turn on the question
whether the local authority is acting *ultra vires*. Not that the citizen
will often be wanting a court order against the members of the
council: normally he will be seeking simply to advance his own
interests and protect his own property in the face of some order by
the council or some refusal by the council to grant him a permission
or licence. Let us examine in rather more detail the range of legal
proceedings which a citizen can initiate against local authorities.

[6] The court will not make these orders if it is satisfied that the member was
acting reasonably or in the belief that the expenditure was authorized by law, and
in any other case the court must have regard to all the circumstances including the
member's means or ability to repay: Local Government Act 1972, s.161 (3).

Here it is the aim of the courts, not to stultify the initiative or to fetter the discretion of local councils, but to see that the legally defined balance between central government, local government, and the governed citizen is maintained consistently with the basic principles of our law and in the way intended by Parliament.

The means whereby a citizen can initiate court proceedings against a local authority are various and increasing. We have already noticed the way in which an elector can challenge the accounts. That method of initiating proceedings is specially provided for by statute, as are various rights of appeal to the courts. To take one example among many, a county council may serve on the owner of any waste land a notice requiring him to maintain it in a proper condition; and the person on whom the notice is served may appeal to the magistrates' court against that notice, either on the ground that it was *ultra vires* (because the land is not waste land or is not within the area of the council's jurisdiction) or on the ground that his land is in a proper condition, or on other grounds specified in the Town and Country Planning Act of 1971. More commonly, statutes provide that appeal against a local authority decision lies first to a minister and then from his decision to the Queen's Bench Division of the High Court (but only on points of law, not on questions of fact or on the merits of the case).

There is never a right of appeal, in the strict sense of appeal, unless a statute expressly provides for it. But if a decision or action of a local authority or a minister is *ultra vires* there is always in principle a remedy in the courts. First, any person whose rights or interests are sufficiently affected may apply to the High Court for a *declaration* that a decision or action is unlawful; such a declaration cannot be enforced against the authority, but it will always be respected as an authoritative determination of the legal rights and wrongs of the matter. Secondly, any person whose rights are directly affected by actual or imminent activity of a local authority may apply to the High Court for an *injunction* ordering the local authority not to proceed unlawfully with that activity; and any member, officer, servant, or agent of the authority who disobeys an injunction risks imprisonment for contempt of court. The same penalty awaits anyone who wilfully fails to comply with an order of *mandamus*, a 'prerogative order' which an interested person may seek from the Queen's Bench Division of the High Court and which requires the authority to perform some duty imposed on it by statute. So that is a third type of remedy. With it go the other prerogative orders, called *certiorari* (by which the Queen's Bench Division quashes a quasi-judicial decision of an authority: for example, a decision to withdraw a licence or to dismiss a public official) and *prohibition* (which orders the authority not to proceed any further with some uncompleted quasi-judicial process of decision-making).

Not everybody in a local government area can make use of these ways of initiating court proceedings in every particular case. Declarations and injunctions were invented and developed by the courts mainly for purposes of litigation between private persons; hence they are in general only available to someone whose own private rights are directly and significantly affected by the acts of the local authority—though sometimes the courts have stretched a point, as for example in 1955 when a ratepayer succeeded in getting a declaration that it was unlawful for a corporation to provide free travel on its omnibuses for old people.[7] (As a result, a special statute was enacted to validate such schemes of travel concession.) The prerogative orders, on the other hand, were devised by the courts as remedies against the abuse of public powers, and so are in principle available to any member of the public in the area who can show that he has any special status or property sufficient to give him an objectively recognizable interest in the proper exercise of the local authority's powers over the matter in question.

The courts will normally require a more substantial interest in the applicant for mandamus than for certiorari or prohibition, but again they are occasionally willing to stretch a point for the sake of preventing abuse of power—and thus ratepayers in 1970 obtained mandamus to require a council to abide by its own standing orders about tendering for contracts.[8] Further, citizens who lack legal rights or special interests sufficient to entitle them either to the private law or to the public remedies, can still go to the Attorney-General and ask him to lend his name to what is called a relator action (nominally by the Attorney-General, on the 'relation' of the citizen) against the local authority.

If the Attorney-General agrees, as he quite often does (for the sake of testing and upholding the law impartially), the legal proceedings will be at the citizen's expense but may be for any of the remedies we have mentioned. And we may notice in passing that there are many situations in which the local authority itself has no right to sue for an injunction (for example, to restrain someone who

[7] *Prescott* v. *Birmingham Corporation* [1955] Ch. 210.
[8] *R.* v. *Hereford Corporation, ex parte Harrower* [1970] 3 All E.R. 460.

persistently breaks and defies the authority's by-laws)[9] but must ask the Attorney-General to seek the injunction in a relator action.

THE PRINCIPLES OF PROCEDURAL FAIRNESS

In a statutory appeal, the court may often (though by no means always, and scarcely ever where the appeal is to the High Court rather than to the magistrates or the county court) have jurisdiction to review not only the power of the authority to make the decision appealed from but also the merits of the decision itself. However, where judicial review is by way of proceedings in the High Court for declaration or any of the prerogative orders, the court can review, not the merits, but only the legality of the decision itself. Still, as we shall shortly see, the High Court can take a broad view of what legality requires: it can and perhaps increasingly does regard decisions and actions of local authorities as *ultra vires* or in some other way unlawful and invalid, not only when the members failed to act in accordance with the formal requirements of the decision-making procedure, or when those members dealt with matters not entrusted to the local authority, but when they acted unfairly, or exercised a discretion quite unreasonably or in a manner repugnant to the general aims of the empowering statute.

First then as to procedure. Many formal statutory requirements as to the composition and procedure of local councils are enforceable by the courts either against the council itself (by mandamus) or against the members. Thus a member who votes on a contract in which he has a pecuniary interest may be prosecuted, and any local elector may institute proceedings in the High Court for declaration, injunction, and order of forfeiture against a person wrongly claiming to be a member. But failure to comply with these very same requirements need not, and quite often does not, render a decision or action of the council *ultra vires* and invalid. And some other statutory requirements cannot be enforced in the courts at all: they are 'directory', not 'mandatory'. But there are certain requirements as to procedure which are laid down in no statute, regulation or standing order, but which are laid down by the courts themselves and must be respected if the validity of a decision or action is to be safe from challenge by any aggrieved person.

The primary procedural requirement insisted on by the courts is

[9] Like Mr. and Mrs. Harris, who were convicted 237 times of illegally selling flowers: *Attorney-General (ex rel. Manchester Corporation)* v. *Harris* [1961] 1 Q.B. 721.

simply this: that decision-making be fair. The concept of fairness is of course a variable and flexible one. The courts tend to think in terms of two basic requirements: that decisions directly affecting a particular man's interests should not be taken without affording him an opportunity to state his case; and that persons with a direct personal interest in a particular decision should not participate in the decision-making.

But fairness extends beyond these two requirements. Thus, where a council assured a local taxi-owners' association that no decision to increase the number of taxi licences would be taken without first consulting the association, the association was held to be entitled to an order of prohibition, so as to prevent the local authority from acting contrary to their assurances; for although the council's assurances had no legal force of themselves, to go back on them was unfair.[10]

Further, the two requirements—fair hearing and lack of bias— are themselves different in different situations. When a council is affecting people's rights by legislative means such as making by-laws, these two general requirements do not apply at all (though the courts supervise by-laws in other ways, as we shall see). But the more a council's decision resembles a judicial decision, and the more it concerns a particular man's status or property or livelihood, or casts a slur on his character or conduct, the more stringent will the courts be in requiring both (i) that a fair opportunity should be given for learning the man's case: for example, before demolishing his house on the ground that he built it without proper notice or consents;[11] and (ii) that the body making the decision should be unbiased: for example, a subcommittee of a council, when meeting to decide whether or not to prohibit the dismissal of a teacher, must not contain members who are governors of the school which dismissed him, even if those governors took no part in the school's decision to dismiss.[12]

THE PRINCIPLES OF LEGALITY AND REASONABLENESS

Beyond procedure there is the question whether the decision itself

[10] R. v. *Liverpool Corporation, ex parte Liverpool Taxi Fleet Operators Association* [1972] 2 Q.B. 299.

[11] Cf. *Cooper* v. *Wandsworth Board of Works* (1863) 14 C.B.(N.S.) 180 (the statute under which the local authority acted has been repealed, but the case remains classical).

[12] *Hannam* v. *Bradford City Council* [1970] 2 All E.R. 690.

is within the local authority's powers. This question can be asked of legislative as well as of administrative and judicial decisions of the authority. Thus the by-laws and traffic regulations made by a local authority must, like the terms and conditions it stipulates in granting planning permission, be sufficiently related to matters which the authority has power so to deal with, and must moreover be consistent with the general law of the land and not repugnant to the objects and sense of the empowering legislation itself; they must be clear and precise, and must not be manifestly unjust, capricious, discriminatory, or oppressive. For example, a by-law requiring an open space to be left behind every new building will be declared invalid by the courts, on the grounds of its capricious unreasonableness, in so far as it concerns a new wing built on to the front of an old building.[13]

But the courts construe by-laws benevolently, not wishing to substitute their own conceptions of prudence and convenience for those of elected representatives of the local people. Much the same may be said of the courts' approach to other decisions and actions of local authorities. Usually the court's judgement that a decision or action is *ultra vires* and invalid will be based, not so much on unreasonableness in a general sense, as on some more indisputable form of excess or abuse of power. Thus, if a local authority is empowered to operate a wash-house (where people wash their own clothes) it is not thereby empowered to run a laundry where clothes are washed by the council's employees.[14] If it is empowered to acquire land compulsorily for slum clearance or coastal protection, it cannot use those powers to acquire land for purposes of speculation or to build a seaside promenade.[15] If it is empowered to exercise its discretion in the public interest it must not abdicate its discretion either by handing over its powers to any other person or body[16] or by adopting policies so rigid as to preclude consideration of any individual circumstances or contentions. Thus, a local authority empowered to license cinemas subject to conditions may not impose a condition that every film shown in the cinema carry the approval of the

[13] *Repton School Governors* v. *Repton Rural District Council* [1918] 2 K.B. 113.

[14] *Attorney-General* v. *Fulham Corporation* [1921] 1 Ch. 440.

[15] *Sydney Municipal Council* v. *Campbell* [1925] A.C. 338; *Webb* v. *Minister of Housing and Local Government* [1965] 2 All E.R. 193.

[16] However, subject to statutory provisions, a local authority may now arrange for the discharge of any of its functions by a committee or subcommittee or officer of the authority or by any other local authority: Local Government Act 1972, s.101 (1).

British Board of Film Censors; for that condition simply substitutes the board's discretion for the local council's.[17] Likewise, to use an inflexible 'first come first served' system of granting licences—whether for cinemas, street-trading stalls, or anything else—may be invalid; it is too arbitrary, and transfers power to the post office and the secretaries who open the mail.[18] And even the broadest discretionary power must not be used so as to frustrate the objects of the statute which conferred it: the obligation of a local authority under the Housing Finance Act of 1972 to raise the rents of council houses is not validly discharged by raising the rent of one unoccupied council house by £18,000 a week.[19]

Inevitably there are occasions when the courts wish to say that an exercise of discretion is so unreasonable, in a more general sense, that it must be held to be *ultra vires*. When this happens there will also inevitably be controversy about the proper division of functions between the local council and the courts, the political process and the law. Two such cases were mentioned in the last chapter. In one the House of Lords, in its judicial capacity, reversed the Court of Appeal's judgement and upheld the High Court's judgement that wages paid by the Poplar Borough Council (which was moved by socialist and feminist principles at a time of unequal and falling wages for men and women) were so excessive as to amount to something other than 'wages'; to the extent of the excess, the wages were declared unlawful and the councillors who voted for them were ordered to repay them to the council out of their own pockets.[20] It made no difference, in the view of the judges, that the statutory power was to pay 'such wages as the council may think fit'. Likewise in 1960 the St. Pancras Borough Council was held to have acted *ultra vires* in refusing, as a matter of political principle, to review and reduce the level of subsidies it was paying to keep down certain rents in the area.[21] To pay some such subsidies was within its powers; but at a certain point the level of payments became, in the judgement of the court, inconsistent with the council's duty to its ratepayers.

This source of tension between councils and courts is not really removed by the statutory power, first conferred on local authorities

[17] *Ellis* v. *Dubowski* [1921] 3 K.B. 621; cf. *Mills* v. *L.C.C.* [1925] 1 K.B. 213.
[18] *Perilly* v. *Tower Hamlets Borough Council* [1972] 3 All E.R. 513.
[19] *Backhouse* v. *Lambeth London Borough Council, The Times*, 14 Oct. 1972.
[20] *Roberts* v. *Hopwood* [1925] A.C. 578.
[21] *Taylor* v. *Munrow* [1960] 1 All E.R. 455.

in 1963, to incur expenditure (since 1974, up to an annual amount not exceeding the product of a twopenny rate) which 'in their opinion is in the interests of their area or any part of it or all or some of its inhabitants'. For although this power is very broad indeed, it does not itself enable the authorities to incur any expenditure 'for a purpose for which they are, either unconditionally or subject to any limitation or to the satisfaction of any condition, authorised or required to make any payment by or by virtue of any other enactment'. So the new free-floating power is not unanchored, and (had it existed at the time) would not, it seems, have served as a life-raft for the councillors of Poplar or St. Pancras shipwrecked on the shoals of judicial review.

We have mentioned only a few of the many cases and contexts in which the citizen may resort to the courts against his local council or councillors. There is little doubt that more recourse has been had to the courts during recent decades. Despite the increasing number of remedies available by way of appeal to ministers or complaint to magistrates, the old High Court remedies are still often used. Whereas only ten orders of mandamus were issued in the period 1964–6, eighteen were issued in 1969, and another fifty-eight applications for leave to apply for it were made. Since the last war the High Court has markedly broadened the availability of certiorari and has shown a new readiness to use the declaration as a public remedy. In the 1960s there was more than a whiff of judicial activism and a revived willingness of the courts to enforce basic principles of fairness and reasonableness against the bearers of statutory authority, whether corporate or individual, local or central, subordinate or ministerial.

No doubt there is much that could be done to simplify the archaic complexity of the various judicial remedies and to clarify the basic principles of what is now called, as for so long it has been called in France, 'administrative law'. The extension of legal aid has done much to bring judicial remedies within the reach of ordinary citizens. New efforts to secure openness, fairness, and impartiality in planning decisions and appeals have also gone some way to familiarize the citizen with the idea that in his dealings with governors and administrators he is usually entitled to 'his day in court' and that 'court' (whether court, tribunal, or inspector) need not be too daunting or expensive. Perhaps the creation of a new administrative division of the High Court, as has been pioneered (like the ombudsman in the English-speaking world) by New Zealand, would compound the advance in all these respects.

As always the problem is one of balance. Courts and their proceedings will always and everywhere entail delay and expense; impartiality is secured at the price of a fully rounded view of disputes in all their origins and context; the judicial virtues are the virtues of men who are not elected and are usually not rooted in the locality. But when all that has been said, the conclusion still remains that in maintaining the balance of legality and fair dealing between central and local government, and between central and local government and the citizen, the co-operation of the courts is, and will continue to be, indispensable. Actual frequency of resort to the courts is a less important influence than the salutary awareness that each of the parties to the partnership of governing and being governed has a real opportunity of taking his case to another forum, in which the conduct of all is open to principled scrutiny and rectification.

11
Present Prospects

THERE are at least three reasons for believing local government has real importance to the England of 1974.

First, it is the complement of Parliament and the only other institution of representative government that citizens possess. After Parliament, therefore, it is the main instrument of English democracy.

Secondly, it is the principal means whereby the national community seeks to meet some of its essential needs: its need for security, through police and fire services; its need for education, for housing, for mobility by road; its need to plan protect and cherish the environment, to promote the welfare of the disadvantaged, and to offer opportunities of recreation for all in leisure time. True, there are nowadays great public services for which local government is *not* responsible. In the welfare field there is the National Health Service and the work of the Social Security and Employment Departments; for public services of convenience there are national or regional bodies for railways, ports, and civil aviation, electricity, gas, water, coal, and steel, telephones, broadcasting, and television. It is also true that for welfare, both inside and outside local government, the country depends greatly on the work of volunteers and voluntary bodies that retain their unofficial character however closely they collaborate with housing, health, and other public authorities. But it remains true none the less that England still looks to local government as a main provider of public services for the protection, welfare, and convenience of the citizen throughout his life.

Thirdly, local government gives expression to the diversity of national life and the desire of local people to work out their own patterns of community. Within the framework of national policy and minimum standards, it enables people grouped in village, town, and county to take decisions for themselves, settle some of their own priorities, spending more than other groups on this and less on that, and generally maintain the special character of different parts of England. Here are a few examples.

This parish council gets a bus shelter put up in the right place, and has the local rights of way sign-posted. This borough fosters 'community development' through officers whose special job is to get closer understanding between groups of local neighbours and the council. That borough experimented with a free family planning service—but only till 1974 when local government lost this power to the new National Health Service. As political power passes from one group to another in this county council, parents find their child no longer eligible for a free place in the direct-grant grammar school —until, after a further shift of power, the council reverses its decision against the grammar school. Here, say at Thornaby on Teesside, an imaginative scheme is launched which offers local citizens with athletic, social, or artistic tastes a range of varied opportunities in a single recreation centre. A district council tackles its housing problem here by building high blocks of flats, there by a scheme which lets each tenant have his own garden. Here council tenants are allowed to buy their houses, there they are not. Here whole areas are cleared of their existing buildings and new houses put up at a distance; here the old houses are improved and the community of local residents escapes disruption.

The fact is that when local power changes hands there can be dramatic effects on a whole range of services: slum clearance, conservation, and redevelopment; school organization, the youth service, and adult education; personal help for families in trouble, the elderly, the mentally distressed; road policy and the balance between private cars and public transport. One obvious result of all such local freedom is a substantial variation in the financial burden placed on ratepayers. Though more than half a council's total expenditure may be met by central grants-in-aid subscribed by national taxpayers, the rates levied by different councils vary between very wide limits, reflecting not only the extent to which needs differ from one area to another but also the differing readiness of councillors, from one place and from one time to another, to make demands on those they represent.

What, then, are the prospects for English local government as the new system comes into operation in 1974? What chance has it of coping successfully with the social and economic changes that will come before the end of the century, at a speed probably even faster than during its first three quarters? In particular, what success will it have in solving present outstanding problems—of housing people properly whatever their incomes, of lifelong education, of transport, and of reconciling claims of 'development' in all its various forms with those of peace and quiet?

Again, will it engage the interest of more or fewer people? Will it be entrusted by Parliament and central government with more or fewer powers? Will it in consequence become more, or less, significant a part of English democratic life? And in the process will it give the country better or worse value for the money it spends out of the pockets of the citizen? How far will it succeed in helping to reconcile freedom with efficiency?

RESPONSE TO THE CHALLENGE OF CHANGE

Here prospects are now somewhat brighter than before 1974. At last England has a permanent device, in the Local Government Boundary Commission, ready to complete the 1972 process of reorganization, keep it under review as circumstances change and experience shows the need for boundary alteration, and recommend accordingly. Further, it seems likely that successive governments will follow the practice of accepting what the commission recommends save in exceptional cases that could be clearly justified. In this way county, district, and parish boundaries will be corrected, and neighbouring areas can be brought together when this seems likely to bring advantage to their inhabitants. Proposals for major changes, say for the creation of a new metropolitan county, can be made by the commission to the Secretary of State and, if he thinks fit, brought by him to Parliament for action. All this is clear gain.

Meanwhile the new counties, no longer divided into autonomous town and country parts, are in a much better position than their predecessors to study social and economic trends and movements throughout continuous geographic areas, and work out for public discussion and decision broad plans of future land-use, covering not only the development of new and old settlements but all aspects of transport, industry, commerce, and the social services. Studying the more detailed implication of these structure plans and giving positive effect to them, especially in housing, will be the responsibility of the districts, and success will here depend on close collaboration between them and the county. This will unquestionably be hard to win: for example, where the district was till yesterday an independent county borough, today has a council dominated by one political group, and yet is part of a new county with a council dominated by that group's opponents. But here is no reason for despair. The new law is flexible. Even the agency arrangements that can be made between county and district may prove helpful. No one pretends the agency relationship is ideal or will work perfectly, but with goodwill it can be varied and improved by trial and error. The fact is that whatever the representative machinery may be, there will inevitably be conflict between different groups of citizen on many issues. There can be no escape, therefore, from the fundamental question: when there is conflict, where does the community, or public, interest lie? Will it prevail when it conflicts with the separate vested interest either of county or of district?

In two further respects local government is now rather better placed to respond to change than before 1974. First, when a council decides that those it represents would benefit from a new service for which the present law makes no provision, it can spend the product of a two-penny rate in securing the provision of that service—if it has confidence that the local ratepayers are prepared to pay and will not show disapproval at the next election. This quite substantial increase in a general power first given to local government in 1963 may prove important. Even the more limited power was used by some imaginative councils to do useful and unusual things: a parish council, for example, stocked the local stream with trout. In future the council of a district such as Warrington (with a population of 163,000) could spend £350,000 a year, or such as Congleton (with 73,000) £160,000, and this scale of expenditure would go some way to brighten many parts of England with new imaginative local schemes for the environment, the arts, or recreation. Indeed, councils could spend much more if the Secretary of State would use his power to increase the two-penny limit, as he could do by order (if his cabinet colleagues agreed) without amendment of the statute.

The second advantage in flexibility that the new councils have over the old concerns internal organization. Though they still have to appoint committees for police, education, and the social services, they are free to adapt their committee structure at any time in any way they like. And though they have to satisfy central government over the appointment of policemen and the heads of their fire, education, and social service departments, they are quite free to appoint other members of their paid staff as experience and changing circumstances suggest they should—and to dis-appoint them too, subject of course to whatever conditions of service have been mutually agreed.

FUTURE SCOPE OF LOCAL GOVERNMENT

Parliament decides the scope of local representative democracy and constantly changes its mind. The functions of local government are therefore in a fairly continuous state of flux. The post-war Labour Government and its parliamentary majority withdrew from local government responsibility for gas, electricity, and hospitals, transferring these services to a new centralized public sector, each under its own pattern of non-elected regional public boards quite unrelated to local government. Another Labour Government (of 1964–70) proposed to withdraw a further slice of local government—community health—and include it with hospitals and doctors in a new pattern of non-elected bodies, related geographically (but not constitutionally) to a reformed local government system. The Conservative Government that followed in 1970 complemented what the Conservatives had done in 1963 for Greater London by reorganizing the rest of English (and Welsh) local government, declaring in the process that this was done to increase its strength. But this same Government withdrew from local government, as the preceding Labour one had proposed, the community health service in order to complete a new comprehensive national system. It also withdrew all services based on water, reorganizing the conservation and supply of water, river pollution, sewage-disposal, and the rest under new non-elected regional water authorities. Thus the G.L.C., within ten years of its creation by one Conservative Government as a great new organ of self-government for 8,000,000 citizens, found itself forced by the next Conservative one to hand over its highly efficient ambulance service and all responsibility for drains and sewers. Only after tough parliamentary in-fighting could it retain its 'water-recreation' duties for the London area.

These reductions in the scope of local self-government were not due to the alleged incompetence of those who worked the old system. Nor are they any proof of central government mistrust of local democrats. They stem from experience and from judgement of a more-than-local public interest. To give one example: is it reasonable to expect the ratepayers of a city mid-stream on the Thames to spend large enough sums installing plant to purify the local sewage effluent before discharge into the river so thoroughly that citizens downstream can safely use the water? 'Yes' was the assumption underlying the old system. But is it not much more reasonable to assume the answer 'no' and transfer responsibility, for both decision and finance, to some body with jurisdiction over the whole length of the Thames? Even so, the major question remains: where does this process of withdrawing functions from the sphere of local government stop?

Should the police follow gas, electricity, hospitals, ambulances, community health, water, and sewage? London has always been an exception to the rule of local democratic responsibility for police, for reasons easy to recognize in a metropolis that is the seat of government. But modern crime knows no geographic boundaries; since 1966 the limits of a police authority have, more often than not, embraced more than the area of one local council; already a powerful dissenting memorandum signed by one member of the Royal Commission on the Police has advocated a national system.[1]

Again, how long will local government remain the main provider of education? It has never been responsible for direct public aid to universities: that comes from central government, uniquely channelled through the University Grants Committee from the Department of Education and Science. But the fees and maintenance of university students are paid by local government, mainly on scales prescribed by central government and with some 90 per cent of the cost met by central grant-in-aid. Often there is great value in the personal link retained under the present system between local authority and student, but here again it can be argued that, more logically, central government should take over the whole relationship between universities and the state.

On present plans for 1981 the total number of students working for degrees will be divided half and half between the universities and polytechnics. The latter are the responsibility of county and metropolitan district councils, and there are strong arguments for

[1] Royal Commission on the Police, *Final Report*, Cmnd. 1728 (H.M.S.O.,1962).

this 'binary' system which keeps under one local government control not only the polytechnics but all other colleges of further whole- and part-time education (technical, commercial, art, adult, and teacher-training). But will the distinction be maintained? There is at least the possibility that central government will replace the binary system with some comprehensive scheme, on a national or regional scale, which would take polytechnics out of local government.

Even at school level the present position of local government can be questioned. Far the largest part of total expenditure is for teachers. Each local council must conform to national salary scales. These are negotiated between representatives of teachers and councils in the Burnham Committee, and require approval by central government. Each local council has some discretion on staffing questions, such as a school's quota of posts of 'special responsibility', but the question is sometimes asked: why not transfer responsibility for this whole salary payment to the centre?

Whatever changes may come in the scope of local government, a long-standing question remains and will become increasingly significant: how is local representative self-government to relate itself in practice to other separate organs of local administration— the regional and area health authorities, the regional water authorities and the rest? Whether or not there are good reasons for the existence of these bodies, they are not representative of local communities as local government councils are meant to be. They add new dimensions to the complexity of government with which the citizen must come to terms. They are a challenge to the local council which seeks to serve the whole community that it represents, to settle its priorities and mobilize its resources of money and manpower. Some form of regional organization might help to bring coherent resolution of these complex problems.

REGIONALISM

There has never been a single regional level of government throughout England, intermediate between local and central authorities. No one can do more than speculate about the prospects of one emerging before the end of the century but there are good grounds for expecting some significant developments.

From the earliest days of Britain's membership of the Common Market she has laid emphasis on the importance of developing those provisions in the Treaty of Rome which enable Western Europe to mobilize its resources in aid of regions that have special needs. Here is one reason for putting Britain's own regional house in better order. Under the stress of mass unemployment in parts of the country before the last war, legislation enabled areas to be designated 'distressed' and to receive special help of various kinds. After the war much more was done to encourage the distribution of industry and economic growth with special areas in mind. But almost all the various efforts of successive governments to this end relied on incentives and disincentives (the grant or withholding of industrial development certificates, investment allowances, Selective Employment Tax, etc.) devised and administered by central rather than by local government. The regional economic planning councils established in the 1960s still have all their chairmen and members appointed by ministers, though local authorities have always been able to suggest candidates for appointment. Nor have these councils any but advisory powers. Local government has been responsible for 'planning' but this has in practice meant planning only of 'land-use' rather than something wide enough to include the whole economic and social spectrum. The Redcliffe-Maud Commission deplored this traditional limitation and proposed the establishment, in areas corresponding closely to the present planning council regions, of eight provincial councils with responsibility for strategic planning in the wider sense.

These councils would be demonstrably rooted in local government. Their membership would chiefly consist of representatives chosen by the main elected councils of the region, together with members co-opted from industry, the trade unions, universities, etc., and they would each elect their own chairman.

These proposals were neither accepted nor rejected either by the Labour or Conservative Government in putting forward plans for local government reform, on the ground that the Crowther–Kilbrandon Commission on the Constitution had not yet reported.[2] The case for provincial councils of some sort would certainly be strengthened if it were decided to decentralize functions now carried out by government in London. As it is, the Trade and Industry, Employment, Environment, and Health and Social Security departments each have regional offices, and their chief officers already form regional boards which service the economic planning councils. The Redcliffe-Maud Commission envisaged the provincial councils as a forum, among other purposes, for continuous

---

[2] The commission reported in October 1973, the majority supporting such proposals, Cmnd. 5460.

discussion on questions of common interest betweeen central and local government, and the value of this role would be proportionately enhanced if central departments upgraded their regional representatives and delegated more authority to them.

But quite apart from helping to relieve congestion in Whitehall provincial councils are now more certainly needed for local purposes than they would have been if local government reform had followed more closely the lines proposed by the Redcliffe-Maud Commission. This is particularly clear in the metropolitan areas. The boundaries of Merseyside, Greater Manchester, and the West Midlands have been far more narrowly drawn by the 1972 act than by the commission.[3] In restricting them to continuously built-up areas the Government claimed as justification that the geographic extent of their potential influence was far too large to serve as the basis of their definition as units of local government, and that such problems as overspill and transportation must therefore be solved by collaboration between neighbouring authorities within a regional context. There can indeed be now no doubt that if the housing and other planning problems of the north-west and the west midlands are to be solved, the new counties of Lancashire, Cheshire, Staffordshire, Hereford and Worcester, Salop, and Warwickshire must reach agreement with the metropolitan authorities that they surround. If such agreement cannot be reached through local government, decisions will have to be imposed by ministers—something which local government reform was intended to make less necessary. The chances of local agreement would surely be much improved by the establishment of provincial councils, representing all the local authorities of a region.

Other arguments in favour of such councils are derived from the legislation for water and for the National Health Service that has been passed since the Royal Commission reported. The Regional Water Authorities (R.W.A.s) cover huge areas based on the course of rivers and therefore often bearing no close relationship to other regional boundaries. But every part of their work is intimately related to local government. That is why a majority of their members are representatives of county and district councils, and why the law enables them—and for some purposes enjoins them—to delegate much of their work to local authorities, acting individually or together. In some parts of the country provincial councils would be

---

[3] Map 1 on pp. 176–7 compares the two sets of boundaries in the case of Merseyside and Greater Manchester.

an excellent means of linking water with local government at regional level.

So, too, they are needed for linking local government with the new National Health Service. As here the pattern is not dictated, like water, by geography, the boundaries have been drawn deliberately to correspond with those of local government. The Area Health Authorities (A.H.A.s) work within boundaries that match those of counties and metropolitan districts, and A.H.A.s are grouped together under Regional Health Authorities (R.H.A.s) which exercise an essential planning and financial function between the secretary of state and the A.H.A.s. It is all the more important that health and local government should work together at regional level because, although at area level the membership of A.H.A.s includes some representatives of local government, the R.H.A.s consist exclusively of central government nominees.

For some years there have been regional advisory councils for further education, providing some common oversight of polytechnics and universities as well as other colleges for students over school age. The 1973 Russell Report on adult education recommended the appointment by all these councils of subcommittees for adult education,[4] and it seems likely that for teacher training and the whole range of higher and other post-school education regional organization will be strengthened in coming years. Whatever form it takes, there would be great advantage if it were brought within the scope of new provincial councils.

Meanwhile the Arts Council of Great Britain has fostered the growth of regional arts associations, especially since the late 1960s, and it has now established its own regional organization throughout England. This is one of the principal means whereby it collaborates with the theatrical, musical, and other artistic activities of local government. During the same period the national Sports Council has organized regional sports councils, bringing together a variety of clubs, voluntary organizations, and local authority representatives, and its provincial patronage is largely distributed as a result of discussion in these bodies. The Countryside Commission as yet has no regional set-up of its own but works through the regional offices of the Environment Department. It should certainly be associated with any provincial councils of the future.

Recreation is likely to prove one of the major growth-points of

[4] Department of Education and Science, *Adult Education: A Plan for Development* (H.M.S.O., 1973), paras. 165–9.

local government activity. Increasing population will itself swell the number of people requiring opportunities for the use of their free time. The amount of that free time will increase as hours of work are shortened, automation reduces demand for many kinds of labour, and growing prosperity reduces the incentive, at least for some people, to work overtime. Already local government offers many very different kinds of opportunity for the use of leisure time: adult education (from flower arrangement to philosophy), libraries, theatres, concerts, opera, art centres and galleries, museums, sports centres, swimming baths, playgrounds, town and country parks, green belts and open spaces. Some councils have in recent years drawn together many of these activities within a single department of recreation, under a single committee (with members co-opted from appropriate outside organizations) and a single officer. But with increasing mobility through public and private motor transport the need for planning and providing for recreation on a regional as well as local scale is constantly becoming greater. Here then is further confirmation of the argument for the provincial council.

Thus the main function of provincial councils would be deliberative, not operational: to be a forum where representatives of neighbouring councils regularly meet each other and where they also meet representatives of central departments, regional health and (where appropriate) water authorities, the regional arts association and sports council, and whatever regional bodies for further, adult, and higher education there may be. Strategic land-use and economic planning of the province, for housing, transport, and development, would be a major subject of discussion; post-school education, the arts, and recreation might be some among many others. They would no doubt work largely through committees, co-opting outside experts for each subject. Their staffs would be appointed by themselves. They might have power to subsidize some projects of provincial interest (as the Redcliffe-Maud Commission recommended) such as an opera house or major sports centre. But their annual expenditure would not be large and they would normally raise it by precept on the authorities represented in their membership.

RELATIONS WITH WHITEHALL

Whatever Parliament's future attitude to local government may prove to be—whether favouring more or less local discretion—what are the prospects of change in the balance of the administrative partnership between central and local authorities? Will the tendency be for councils in practice to become more like, or less like, agents of the centre than sources of independent democratic decision? Will the balance tilt on the side of national uniformity or local diversity?

At present those whose faith is in local democracy must face some unpalatable facts. There is no prospect of councils' acquiring substantial new sources of local taxation: they will be increasingly dependent on central funds to meet rising costs or satisfy demand for new or improved services. Moreover in managing the national economy central government does not hesitate to impose sudden and drastic cuts in approved plans for forward capital expenditure by local councils, sometimes in key sectors such as highway construction, more often still in the non-key sectors where most local discretion lies. Again, growing public interest in decisions affecting the environment encourages ministerial concern with local problems (of planning, conservation, or development) and decisions are taken in London, often after long delay.

On the other hand, ministers of both major political parties constantly assert their faith in local government and their determination to relax all controls but the essential. Certainly the machinery for approving capital-spending plans has been improved and simplified. The oversight of local government planning, housing, and transport has now been absorbed in one Department of the Environment, and this promises some gain for local councils in their relations with Whitehall, though sceptics still prophesy that the unsolved problems of running a mammoth department will end in a return to separate ministries. Meanwhile progress towards corporate management by local councils has not yet been matched by a similar movement at the centre: the Environment, Education, Social Security, and Home Departments, for example, still have their individual styles of life in dealing with local government and call on councils independently for programmes of development starting at different times and covering different numbers of years.

It is too early to say how the new councils will organize their own associations or how effectively they will learn to deal with Whitehall and make common cause.[5] The Redcliffe-Maud Commission

[5] Separate associations have already been formed, one for the metropolitan counties and districts, the G.L.C., and London boroughs; another for the other counties; and a third for the other districts. The Parish Councils Association continues as before 1974.

thought one of the advantages of its proposed single tier of main executive authorities was that at last local government would thus acquire the power of speaking with one voice to central government. That will not happen now. But there are forces in local government that have long worked, and are still working, to consolidate alliance between the various elements. A stronger federal body of the new associations than that contemplated in 1973 may emerge quite soon. On this will certainly depend much of their future strength. Those who believe in local government must greatly hope that they will come to terms with one another and develop quickly their own common services for information and research, recruitment, training, and negotiation.

THE FUTURE LOCAL GOVERNORS

For the future of English local government the single most important element in the whole complex is the quality of the elected councillor, though that of the senior staff which councillors appoint comes a close second. Councillors let contracts, some of them worth many thousands of pounds. They rightly have information (which they *could* use for their own advantage) before this can be made available to the public. They take decisions, many of which intimately affect the lives of individual men women and children at highly sensitive points. No one can seriously use language about a councillor that is often, and at least plausibly, used about the back-bench Member of Parliament: 'He runs nothing, decides nothing and usually knows nothing worth paying for.'[6]

No one can do more than speculate on whether the average quality of English local councillors will improve or deteriorate in coming years. But it is worth considering how far the chances have been affected by recent changes in the system.

Party politics seem certain to play an increasingly important part in local government. In London and the large cities they have dominated the scene for years and their influence will now grow in the new counties and many of the new districts. All three national parties will therefore be bound to take more seriously their search for candidates and their efforts to get them elected and help them in their local government work. The result should be to raise the standard of councillors and widen the social spectrum from which they come.

[6] Mr. Richard Crossman M.P., *The Times*, 4 July 1973, p. 16.

On the other hand, both counties and districts are geographically larger than the old ones. Continuing improvement in means of travel will lessen this disadvantage but the time of meetings will inevitably tend to shift away from the evening and this will make membership of councils still more difficult for younger people and others in full-time work.

How much time a conscientious councillor will have to find for his public work depends largely on the extent to which the council delegates detail to officers and streamlines its committee organization, and partly on the amount of discretion it allows to committee chairmen. It seems at least likely that in future 'back-bench' councillors will not need to spend as much time as their predecessors in the formal, repetitive, or trivial business of subcommittees or committees or in the attempt to master long printed reports or schedules of detailed items. On the other hand, the councillor may well wish to spend time saved from meetings in making himself more available to his constituents. In fact no improvement in organization can substantially reduce the heavy demands of local government on the free time of its practitioners. For reasons mentioned in discussing recreation opportunities above, it can be expected that the people of England will in years to come have more free time. Here there might be an increasingly wide field for local government recruits—though not, unfortunately, from among those of less ripe years, who would be specially welcome and are at present hard to find.

Is one conclusion that elected local governors ought to be paid, and that eventually they will be? Why is no national party at present prepared to say they should be paid, when not only are all elected Members of Parliament paid quite substantial salaries and allowances but part-time members of nationalized industry boards receive four-figure part-time salaries too? The answer is the simple one that public opinion has so far been content to leave things in local government as they have always been. It is now generally accepted that the old crude limitation even on the extent to which local governors could claim repayment of expenses was unfair. Rather more generous allowances for time spent on council matters can now be claimed. Perhaps in time there will also be acceptance of the principle that *some* members of a council should be recognized as carrying responsibilities that demand substantially more time than that required of the other members, and that these councillors should receive a part-time salary comparable to that paid to part-time members of, say, gas or electricity boards. This was recommended unanimously in 1967 by the Maud Committee, which consisted for the most part of members representative of all the various types of council existing at the time and included men of all the main political parties. Nevertheless it must remain a very open question whether at present any system of compensation which seems to distinguish between 'front-bench' and 'back-bench' councillors would be generally acceptable to local governors. In any case it would be wrong to expect that payment of councillors would have more than a marginal effect upon their future quality, whether that effect would be for better or for worse.

More important, perhaps, will be what councils do, at their discretion, to make the working life of their members easier to bear. The allocation of staff to serve as secretaries of the leader of the council (that is, of the majority group), the leader of the opposition (that is, of the minority group), or the chairmen of important committees; provision of secretarial help for other members, telephones, and better accommodation at county or city hall, especially for councillors meeting their constituents—these are among the improvements that have already been introduced in some places and, if they become general, may help to attract into local government more men and women of the calibre required.

In the long run much will depend on future relations between councils, the local and national press, and those responsible for local and national television and broadcasting. Local newspapers have always been invaluable to local government, and always will be. Since local radio started work, it has greatly helped to bridge the gap between citizen and councillor. With rare exceptions, however, national television and broadcasting have helped little and have rather served to confirm the popular view that local government is a dreary subject, with only occasional entertainment value derived from scandal or Victorian music-hall jokes about the mayor.

No doubt this is partly local government's fault. There has been substance in the frequent allegation that English local governors are costive and keep their decision-making to themselves. Recent demands for more open local government are encouraging—and worth encouragement. But much has already been done in many places to make information easily available to public, press, and the mass media. Much more will no doubt be done by the new councils— through the local government information office, local public relations officers, council publication of documents (such as those already published by the G.L.C.) analogous to the consultation and policy papers now commonly issued by central government as a preliminary to legislation, and many other new devices for encouraging genuine discussion between the local governors and the governed.

PARISH AND NEIGHBOURHOOD COUNCILS

Because county and district councils are responsible under the 1972 act for the main local government services, the English system is naturally described as a two-tier or two-level one. But its future success partly depends on what might be called the third estate: the level of councils underlying that of the district and the county. Before 1974 this level in all rural areas consisted of parish councils and parish meetings. These alone of all types of local authority survived the holocaust of 1972, and their powers are now greater than before. Further, many of the old boroughs and urban districts now absorbed in larger areas have acquired a new independent status, some retaining a town mayor as their chief citizen, with all his dignities preserved, and all possessing an elected council with the same status and powers as a rural parish.

If the Redcliffe-Maud Report had been adopted, these new local councils would have been the sole elected body between the main all-purpose authority and the citizen. Even as it is, they have a role of potentially great importance—a right to be consulted on all planning applications; power to speak for their community, whether advocating or protesting against any cause on which their district or county must make up its mind; to lobby the district or county councillors concerned; and on their own initiative to do anything they think will be in the interest of their locality that is not the statutory business of some other council. Service on these local bodies offers an open door to all good citizens who wish to serve their neighbours in one way or another but lack the time to do so through membership of district or county council—or perhaps hesitate to adopt a party label. It seems likely that before long similar chances of service on local councils will be offered in neighbourhoods within large urban areas, whether the councils be statutory or, as under the new Scottish arrangements, on an unofficial basis. During the passage of the 1972 act through Parliament action of this kind was strongly pressed, by back-bench members and by interests such as the Association for Neighbourhood Councils. The act in consequence enables the Boundary Commission to propose the creation of new parishes and new parish councils during the course of its periodic reviews.

VOLUNTARY ORGANIZATIONS AND THE VOLUNTEER

One of the brightest prospects for the future health of many local services lies in the growing involvement of the British volunteer. Historically, the pattern has often been for a group of voluntary enthusiasts to concern themselves with a particular social problem, pioneer local solutions (say, the community health centre at Peckham), obtain the goodwill of the local council and in due course financial help from it, and find eventually that public opinion expressed itself through Parliament in legislation covering the country. School meals and milk, the work of housing associations and of nursery school enthusiasts, are some of many examples from the pre-war period; the Citizens' Advice Bureau service, now with 560 branches and grants from both central and local government, developed during the war after a series of earlier experiments; family planning, adventure playgrounds, and rural music schools are among the various movements that have followed a similar pattern since 1945.

The Seebohm Committee had no doubt that the expansion of personal social services which it thought necessary called for a huge increase in the involvement of neighbours in their community, however much was also needed from the local council and the state.[7] It seems equally clear that the new system of national health, if it is to serve the patient and avoid the risk of clinical and bureaucratic inhumanity, needs even more support from unofficial volunteers than the old system had from 'Leagues of Friends' attached to scores of individual hospitals. Already thousands of old-style and new-style volunteers support the work of statutory social service and health authorities—visiting the disabled in their homes, supplementing the ambulance and ward services, organizing concerts in hospitals, play groups for children, youth camps, and holidays. If professional social workers and other officers, elected councillors, and appointed members of new health authorities can find the time and imagination to encourage and make full use of this enthusiasm, there is the chance of a great increase over the next few years in both the scope and the humanity of local democratic action.

[7] Cmnd. 3703, paras. 491–500.

LOCAL GOVERNMENT STAFF

What kind of recruits to the paid service of local councils are in future likely to be sought and found? In particular, who will be head of the council's whole paid staff, whether known as clerk, chief executive, or under some other title, and who will be in charge of the council's main departments and therefore members of the top-level team led by the chief officer? What general or specific qualifications will they normally have?

The first appointments made by the new councils elected in 1973 suggest the answer 'much as before'. The council's chief officer will frequently be a lawyer; the treasurer a professional accountant; the chief education officer a university graduate with some first-hand experience of teaching and, for a longer period, of educational administration; the social services department head a man or woman professionally qualified in some branch of social administration and probably a graduate.

But for various reasons the 1973 appointments may not prove valid guides to future practice. Councils had to make them in a hurry and before they had experience of making collective judgements. Moreover, because of the desirability of carrying through reorganization with as few redundancies and as little disturbance to serving officers as possible, no one outside the local government service was eligible for appointment, and while any officer serving outside London could apply for the very top posts (which were advertised on a national scale), for all other appointments councils were bound to give first preference to candidates serving in their own or a neighbouring area. Further, a council's natural tendency to prefer a familiar face to an outside candidate was on this occasion strongly reinforced by the argument that local experience would be invaluable in sorting out the special problems of transition to the new local government system. It was almost inevitable therefore that in 1973 most councils played for safety, appointed local men, and made few innovations in established practice. Even so a few chief executive posts went to men who had no legal training.

More significant as pointing a trend for future top appointments is the wide adoption by new councils of the new type of departmental organization based on the philosophy of corporate management. There is good ground of hope that when councils have emerged from the troubled waters of reorganization and in a few years' time have to make new appointments, they will seek *managers* for their top posts. Professional qualifications of various kinds will certainly still be needed, but there will be greater opportunities for men with graduate and post-graduate education, intellectual ability, and proven skills in handling human relationships with senior and junior colleagues. Further, the top local government officer will be expected to possess political skill of a high order. Like senior members of the home civil service, he will need to know the mind of his political masters in the council, to use his influence in helping them to reach decisions and to make the best of whatever decisions they may take. But whereas the national civil servant has only one political chief (the head of his department) to serve at any one time and normally has none but informal contact with members of the opposition, the local government officer has a collective master (the majority group or party on the council) and must also be prepared to deal with any member of the council who asks him, as a servant of the council, for advice or information.

In consequence of such developments as these, the local government service will offer careers calling for qualities of broader range, more interest and greater challenge than before. Pay, pensions, and conditions of work will continue to be settled mainly through negotiations on a national scale, and they are likely to improve broadly in parallel with central government service and other comparable employment. The quality of future recruits will partly depend on the general reputation of local government: the more important its work is thought to be and the wider the discretion, for better or worse, that people think local governors can exercise, the more attractive to able men and women will the service become as a career.

But much will also depend on the practice followed by councils: in particular on their methods of selection and promotion and on their attitudes to training. How soon, for example, will a woman be appointed to the top post by any major council? Or to the headship of any department other than libraries, social services, or education? How quickly will the practice spread of appointing honours graduates (with degrees in subjects other than science, technology, or law) to other departments than education? How soon will 'generalists', such as those who for years have traditionally had reason to look forward to the highest posts in the home and diplomatic civil services, have evidence that they can hope to become head or deputy head of a local government department? Will promising recruits find encouragement to add to their qualifications in the course of their career, and on secondment from their council attend courses in management and other relevant subjects?

The progress already made by some councils in recent years suggests that the answer to none of these questions need be negative. If the momentum of reform developed over the last ten years and culminating in the 1972 act can be maintained throughout the 1970s, there is a fair prospect that all such questions will in due course receive a favourable answer from the historian of English local government.

THE REPUTE OF ENGLISH LOCAL GOVERNMENT

Good public relations have been well defined as 'good conduct for which you take the credit'. Without good conduct local governors will in the long run certainly get no credit; and about aspects of their conduct—and the credit or discredit due to them—opinions in a democracy are rightly bound to differ. It will always be the more important for local government, therefore, that its conduct is, and is seen to be, without reproach in matters such as integrity and freedom from corruption about which there is a general consensus in society. Here English local government has established standards which probably no other country has excelled: will it maintain and improve upon them?

There have always been, and no doubt there always will be, cases of corruption in English local government. Some of these have led to prosecution in the courts and the conviction of individuals for criminal offences. In 1971, for example, this happened notoriously in Wandsworth, in 1973 in Pontefract; and, in 1973 also, certain prosecutions widely affecting local government in the north-east were begun. The number of such cases represents only a minute fraction of the contracts let, the transactions affecting land and the mass of planning and other decisions taken by local governors day by day. But though very few of these other cases were the subject of court proceedings, were any of them 'improper' without being criminal? Is the fear justified that what has emerged in the courts 'may be no more than an indication of a much deeper disease'?[8]

A councillor is already bound to declare his financial interest in any matter coming before the council and he is forbidden to debate or vote on it except by special permission of the Secretary of State (who seldom grants this, and then only to council tenants when

[8] *The Times*, 18 July 1973, p. 17.

otherwise the conduct of council business would be difficult). The staff of councils are already bound by a strict code of professional conduct which forbids their accepting outside payments without the council's leave. Some councils already take still sterner measures to ensure that councillors make public any of their interests that could be considered relevant, and may be such arrangements will become general.

But by its very nature local government will always attract as candidates persons with business interests in land, commerce, housing and many other subjects with which, if elected councillors, they will still be personally concerned. In efforts to protect their reputation for disinterested service of the public, councils will no doubt experiment with standing orders designed, say, to prevent certain of their members becoming chairmen or members of some committees and to provide that special interests of all councillors shall be entered in a register and open to inspection by the public. Parliament may make similar legislative experiments on local government's behalf. The government of the day may sometime think it right that a commission should investigate some aspect of local government activity and recommend improvements in procedure.[9] But no legislation or administrative device can in the end safeguard the public against dishonesty: only the character of the councillor and the vigilance of his constituents can do that.

About the repute of English local government at any future date there can be no more than speculation. What can be prophesied with certainty is this: the public will not tolerate the sense that its affairs are being run by bureaucrats, whether employed by central or by local governors, however well equipped and qualified. The more mature the English people may become with further development of lifelong education, the more they will insist on feeling able to object or to take positive initiatives when things need to be stopped or to be done. It is inconceivable that they could have this feeling if local government in England withered away. Fortunately there is some reason for believing that a new lease of life and liveliness began for it in 1974.

[9] In October 1973 the Prime Minister appointed a committee, under Lord Redcliffe-Maud's chairmanship, to consider the adequacy of present rules governing the conduct of local authority members and officers in situations where there might be conflict between their position in local government and their private interests, and qualification or disqualification for service as a member of a local authority or of any of its committees; to consider what principles should apply, and to make recommendations regarding compliance with such principles.

Appendix 1

Local authorities: population size

	Population, *1971 census* (*thousands*)						
	0–40	40–75	75–120	120–200	200–500	500–1m.	over 1m.
G.L.C. and Metropolitan counties (7)	–	–	–	–	–	–	7
Non-metropolitan counties (39)	–	–	1	–	11	23	4
London boroughs (33)	1	–	–	9	23	–	–
Metropolitan districts (36)	–	–	–	6	25	4	1
County districts (296)	14	97	144	33	8	–	–
TOTALS (411)	15	97	145	48	67	27	12

Source: *County Councils Gazette*, Jan. 1973.

Appendix 2

Expenditure of English local authorities, 1971-2
(in £ millions)

	Capital	Revenue[1]
Education	295	2,349
Housing	960	931
Police	25	406
Highways	232	388
Water and sewage[2]	234	321
Social services	36	298
Trading services (buses, ports, etc.)	85	245
Public health and refuse	25	172
Local health services[3]	12	133
Fire	8	85
Parks	21	84
Libraries, museums, and galleries	9	75
Planning	70	74
Other services	71	293
General administration	24	390
Totals	£2,107m.	£6,244m.

Notes: (1) Figures exclude expenditure from certain special funds (e.g. super-
annuation fund).
(2) From 1974 the responsibility of regional water authorities.
(3) From 1974 the responsibility of regional and area health authorities.
Source: Department of the Environment, *Local Government Financial Statistics.*
1971-2 (H.M.S.O., 1973).

Select Bibliography

(1) OFFICIAL REPORTS (all published by H.M.S.O.)

Royal Commission on Local Government in Greater London, *Report*, Cmnd. 1164 (1960) (Herbert Report).

Local Government Commission for England, *Reports 1–9*, 1961–5.

Royal Commission on Local Government in England, *Report*, Cmnd. 4040 (1969) (Redcliffe-Maud Report).

Local Government Boundary Commission for England, *Reports 1–6*, 1972–3.

Commission on the Constitution, *Report*, Cmnd. 5460, 1973 (Kilbrandon Report).

Committee on the Management of Local Government, *Report*, 1967 (Maud Report).

Committee on the Staffing of Local Government, *Report*, 1967 (Mallaby Report).

Department of the Environment, *The New Local Authorities: Management and Structure*, 1972 (Bains Report).

Committee on Local Authority and Allied Personal Social Services, *Report*, Cmnd. 3703 (1968) (Seebohm Report).

Department of the Environment, Central Advisory Water Committee, *The future management of water in England and Wales*, 1971.

Department of the Environment, *The Future Shape of Local Government Finance*, Cmnd. 4741 (1971) (Green Paper).

Department of Health and Social Security, *The Future Structure of the National Health Service*, 1970 (Green Paper).

Department of Health and Social Security, *National Health Service Reorganisation*, 1971 (Consultative Document).

House of Lords Select Committee on Sport and Leisure, *Interim* and *Final Reports*, 1973

(2) HISTORY AND THEORY OF LOCAL GOVERNMENT

THORNHILL, W., *The Growth and Reform of English Local Government* (Weidenfeld & Nicolson, 1971).
LIPMAN, V. D., *Local Government Areas 1834–1945* (Blackwell, 1949).
HALSEY, A. H. (ed.), *Trends in British Society since 1900* (Macmillan, 1972), Ch. 9.
WILSON, C. H. (ed.), *Essays in Local Government* (Blackwell, 1948), Ch. 1.
MACKENZIE, W. J. M., *Theories of Local Government* (L.S.E., 1961).
SHARPE, L. J., 'Theories and Values of Local Government', *Political Studies*, 18 no. 2, (June 1970).

(3) STRUCTURE

WISEMAN, H. V. (ed.), *Local Government in England 1958–69* (Routledge & Kegan Paul, 1970).
MORTON, JANE, *The Best Laid Schemes* (Chas. Knight, 1970).
RHODES, G., and RUCK S. K., *The Government of Greater London* (Allen & Unwin, 1970).
SMALLWOOD, F., *Greater London: the politics of metropolitan reform* (Bobbs Merrill, New York, 1965).
RHODES, G. (ed.), *The New Government of London: the first five years* (Weidenfeld & Nicolson, 1972).
WISTRICH, ENID, *Local Government Reorganisation: the first years of Camden* (London Borough of Camden, 1972).
Redcliffe-Maud Commission, *Research Study 2: Lessons of the London Government Reforms* (H.M.S.O., 1968).
JONES, G. W., 'The Local Government Act 1972 and the Redcliffe-Maud Commission', *Political Quarterly*, 44, no. 2 (April 1973).
DOUGLAS, J., 'Four years after Maud', *Municipal Review*, June 1973.

(4) COUNCILS AND THE COMMUNITY

HILL, DILYS, *Participating in Local Affairs* (Penguin, 1970).
REES, A. M. and SMITH, T., *Town Councillors: a study of Barking* (Acton Society Trust, 1964).
HAMPTON, W., *Democracy and Community: a study of politics in Sheffield* (O.U.P., 1970).
SHARPE, L. J. (ed.), *Voting in Cities* (Macmillan, 1967).
COX, H. and MORGAN, D., *City Politics and the Press: journalists and the governing of Merseyside* (Cambridge U.P., 1973).
Maud Report, Volume 2: *The Local Government Councillor*; Volume 3: *The Local Government Elector* (H.M.S.O., 1967).
Redcliffe-Maud Commission, Research Study 9: *Community Attitudes Survey: England* (H.M.S.O., 1969).

Ministry of Housing and Local Government, *People and Planning: Report of the Committee on Public Participation in Planning* (H.M.S.O., 1969) (Skeffington Report).

DRAKE, C. D., 'Ombudsmen for Local Government', *Public Administration*, 48 (Summer 1970).

(5) INTERNAL ORGANIZATION

WISEMAN, H. V., *Local Government at Work* (R.K.P., 1967).

Royal Institute of Public Administration, *Management of Local Government: the Maud Committee Report* (RIPA, 1968).

KNOWLES, R. S. B., *Modern Management in Local Government* (Butterworths, 1971).

LEE, J. M. and WOOD, B., *The Scope of Local Initiative: a study of Cheshire county council 1961–74* (Martin Robertson, 1974).

RIPLEY, B. J., *Administration in Local Authorities* (Butterworths, 1970).

STEWART, J. D., *Management in Local Government: A Viewpoint* (Chas. Knight, 1971).

HEADRICK, T. E., *The Town Clerk in English Local Government* (Allen & Unwin, 1962).

RICHARDS, AUDREY and KUPER, A. (eds.), *Councils in Action* (Cambridge U.P., 1971), pp. 171–201.

DEARLOVE, J., *The Politics of Policy in English Local Government* (Cambridge U.P., 1973).

Maud Report, Volume 5: *Local Government Administration in England and Wales* (H.M.S.O., 1967).

ELLIOTT, J., 'The Harris Experiment in Newcastle upon Tyne', *Public Administration*, 49 (Summer 1971).

CHESTER, D. N., 'Local Democracy and the Internal Organization of Local Authorities', *Public Administration*, 46 (Autumn 1968).

GREENWOOD, R., SMITH, A. D. and STEWART, J. D., 'Corporate Planning and the Chief Officers' Group', *Local Government Studies*, 1 (Oct. 1971).

(6) FINANCE AND CENTRAL-LOCAL RELATIONS

HEPWORTH, N. P., *The Finance of Local Government* (Allen & Unwin, 1970).

Royal Institute of Public Administration, *Sources of Local Revenue* (RIPA, 1968).

GRIFFITH, J. A. G., *Central Departments and Local Authorities* (Allen & Unwin, 1966).

BOADEN, N., *Urban Policy-Making* (Cambridge U.P., 1971).

SHARP, EVELYN, *The Ministry of Housing and Local Government* (Allen & Unwin, 1969).

SWAFFIELD, J. C., 'Local Government in the National Setting', *Public Administration*, 48 (Autumn 1970).

BOADEN, N., 'Central Departments and Local Authorities: the relationship examined', *Political Studies*, 18, no. 2 (June 1970).

(7) LOCAL GOVERNMENT AND THE COURTS

BUXTON, R. J., *Local Government* (Penguin, 2nd ed., 1973).
CROSS, C. A., *Principles of Local Government Law* (Sweet & Maxwell, 4th ed., 1971).
HART, W. O. and GARNER, J. F., *Local Government and Administration* (Butterworths, 9th ed., 1973).
WADE, H. W. R., *Administrative Law* (O.U.P., 3rd ed., 1971).

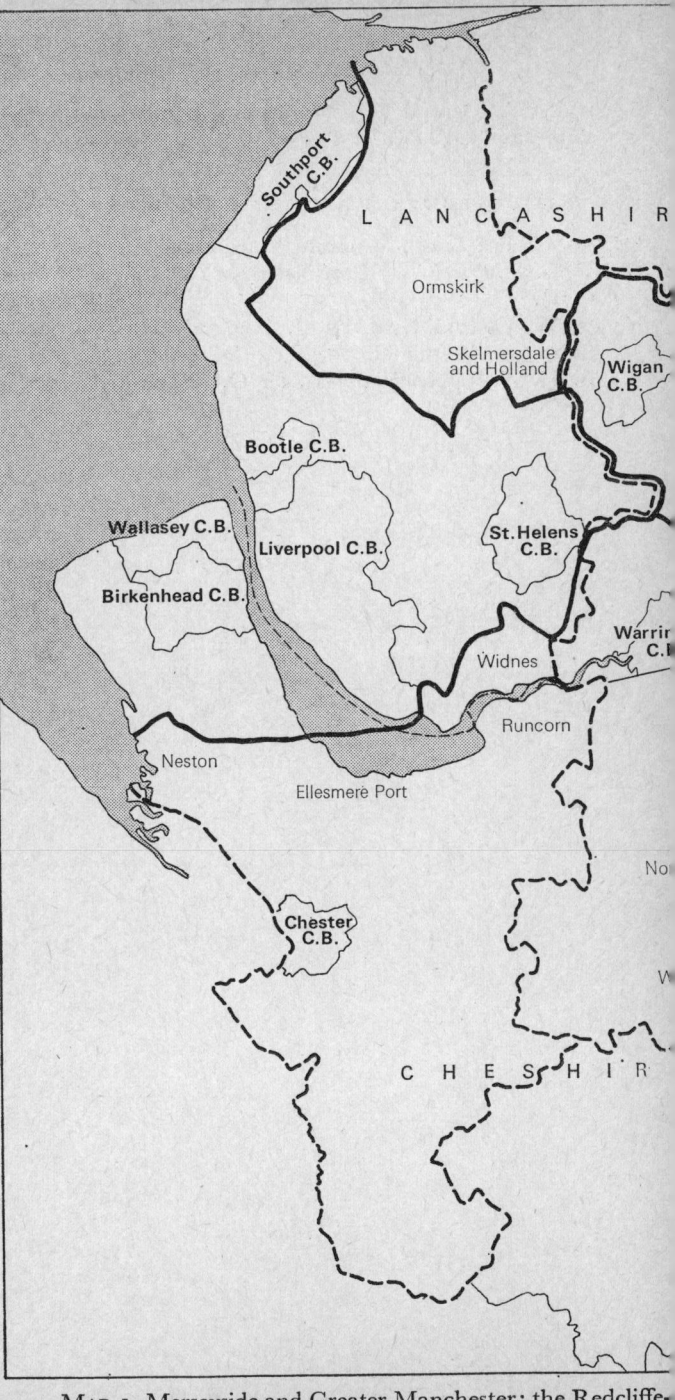

MAP 1. Merseyside and Greater Manchester: the Redcliffe-

Turton

Whitworth

Bolton C.B.

Bury C.B.

Rochdale C.B.

Oldham C.B.

WEST RIDING

Salford C.B.

Manchester C.B.

Stockport C.B.

Glossop

DERBYSHIRE

.ymm

New Mills

Wilmslow

Whaley Bridge

Knutsford

Macclesfield

ddle-
ch

- - - Redcliffe-Mauds' boundaries (1969)
━━━ 1972 Act boundaries
─── Former county and county borough boundaries

0   5   10   15 miles

0   10   20 km

mission and the 1972 act boundaries compared.

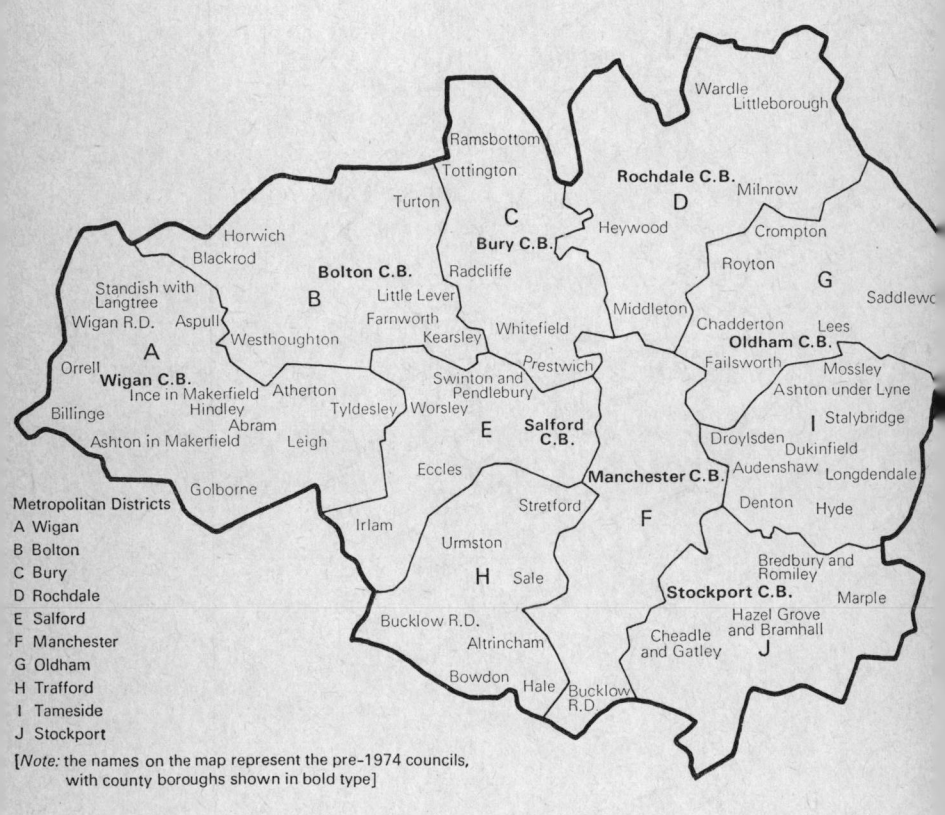

Metropolitan Districts
A Wigan
B Bolton
C Bury
D Rochdale
E Salford
F Manchester
G Oldham
H Trafford
I Tameside
J Stockport

[*Note:* the names on the map represent the pre-1974 councils, with county boroughs shown in bold type]

MAP 2. Metropolitan districts in the county of Greater Manchester.

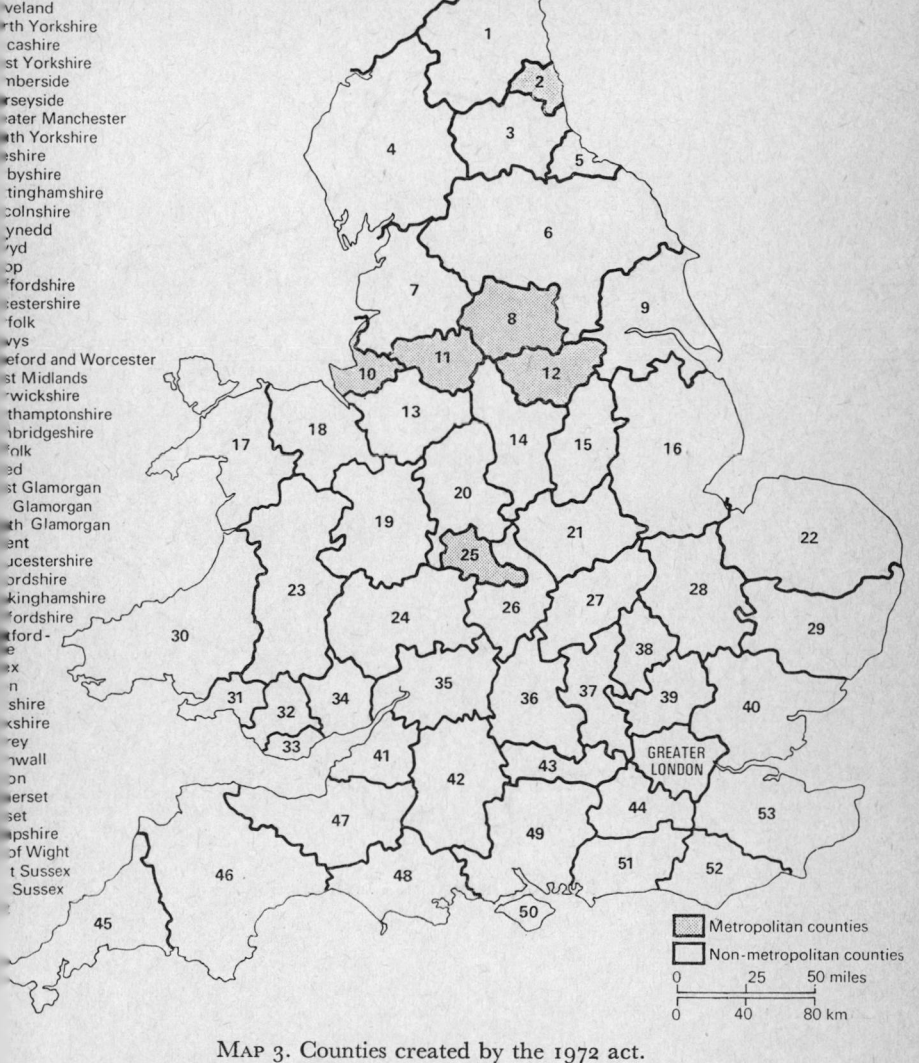

GREATER
LONDON

Metropolitan counties

Non-metropolitan counties

0   25   50 miles

0   40   80 km

MAP 3. Counties created by the 1972 act.

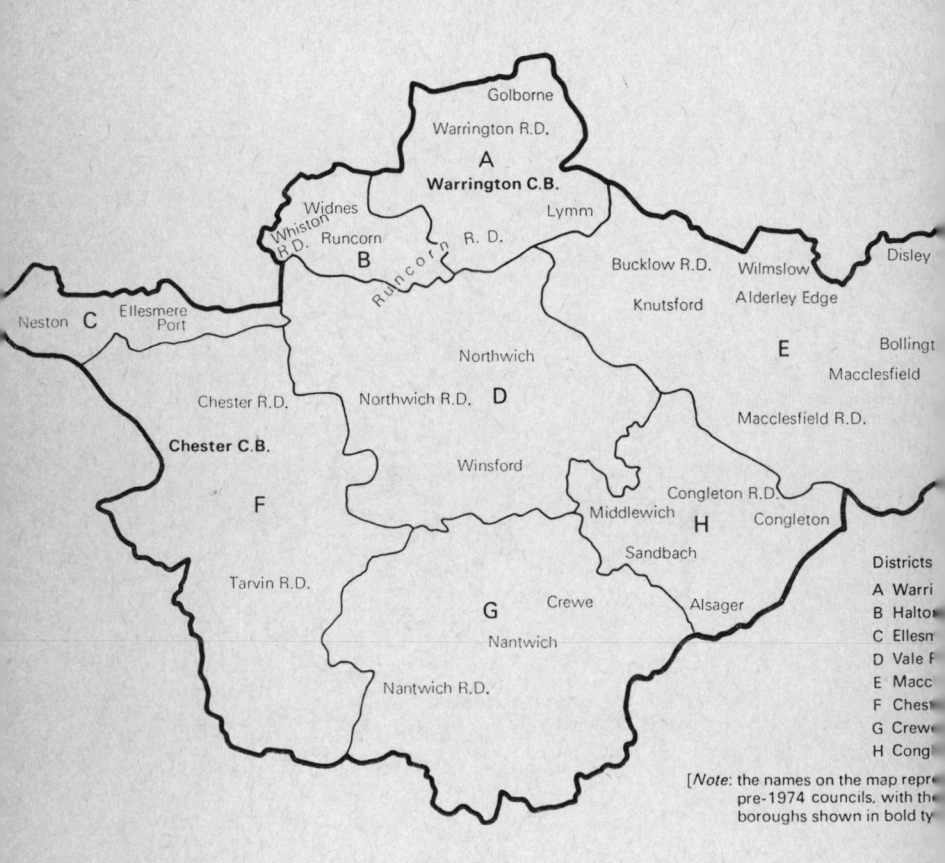

Golborne

Warrington R.D.

A

Warrington C.B.

Widnes

Whiston

R.D. Runcorn

B

Runcorn R.D.

Lymm

Bucklow R.D.

Wilmslow

Disley

Knutsford

Alderley Edge

Neston C

Ellesmere
Port

Northwich

E

Bollingt

Macclesfield

Chester R.D.

Northwich R.D. D

Macclesfield R.D.

Chester C.B.

Winsford

Congleton R.D.

F

Middlewich

H

Congleton

Sandbach

Tarvin R.D.

Crewe

Alsager

G

Nantwich

Nantwich R.D.

Districts

A Warri
B Halto▪
C Ellesm▪
D Vale F
E Macc▪
F Chest▪
G Crew▪
H Congl▪

[*Note*: the names on the map repr▪
pre-1974 councils, with the▪
boroughs shown in bold ty▪

Map 4. Districts in Cheshire.

Index